Deconstructing Prehumanity

An Enquiry into the Archaeological Creation of a Black Past

Jorge Serrano

University Press of America,® Inc.
Lanham • Boulder • New York • Toronto • Plymouth, UK

4501 Forbes Boulevard, Suite 200, Lanham, Maryland 20706
UPA Acquisitions Department (301) 459-3366

Unit A, Whitacre Mews, 26-34 Stannery Street,
London SE11 4AB, United Kingdom

Printed in the United States of America
British Library Cataloguing in Publication Information Available

Library of Congress Control Number: 2014953526
ISBN: 978-0-7618-6357-1 (pbk. : alk. paper)—ISBN: 978-0-7618-6358-8 (electronic)

∞™ The paper used in this publication meets the minimum requirements of American National Standard for Information Sciences Permanence of Paper for Printed Library Materials, ANSI/NISO Z39.48-1992.

For Frances, Harrison, and Nicole

munus amoris et inritamen constantiae datis

Dark daughter of the lotus leaves that watch the
Southern sea,
Wan spirit of a prisoned soul a-panting to be free;
The muttered music of thy streams, the whispers of
the deep
Have kissed each other in God's name and kissed a
world to sleep.

The will of the world is a whistling wind sweeping a
cloud-cast sky,
And not from the east and not from the west knelled its
soul-searing cry;
But out of the past of the Past's gray past, it yelled from
the top of the sky;
Crying: Awake, O ancient race! Wailing: O woman
arise!
And crying and sighing and crying again as a voice
in the midnight cries;
But the burden of white men bore her back, and the
white world stifled her sighs.

excerpt from poem titled "The White Man's Burden"
by W. E. B. Du Bois (in *The Crisis* volume 9: November 1914)

Contents

List of Figures

Preface

I would like to thank all of the people who made this extensive research possible and all of the people who endured my tenacious passion for delving into the roots of things. I also want to especially thank James Pope who flowed with me for a little while in a very big way.

This book is not an extensive history but a perception of how some notions of the past reflect current human social conditions. This is a survey of how the earliest ancestors and human origins intersect with perceptions of an African past. I have focused on the meanings used and looked at past researchers whose work on the origins of humanity can be read as narrative. Like many area studies this one has its share of contentions and rivalries. I have not entered into the Darwinian evolutionism versus creationism dispute but, as with questions about origins, it is there. This work is about several human stories and the search for scientific truth, if such a thing can ever be finite (scientism involves social constructions that are created by people). The data in the form of fossils and their archaeological sites lend themselves to interpretations that comprise of human perceptions no matter how intense claims of objectivity may seem. Paleoanthroplogy, or rather the archaeological reconstructive endeavor of an African past, is at the center of this analysis. My intent is not to vilify any one person or research institution but rather to make known the human processes involved. The Du Boisian model that implicates the many creativities of constructing a *tertium quid* comes in the guise of prehumanity.

Introduction

THE MEANING OF ANTHROPOLOGIZATION

Anthropology as a science of humanity can be construed as measurer of reified cultures (past and present) that are viewed by a spectrum of an enclosed intellectual *milieu*. Ideas extracted from this study of humanity uphold and affect our present social human condition. Science, or as understood here, anthropological analyses have produced descriptive and explanative writings about humanity primarily as an existential portraiture in dyadic form: in other/same and or black/white juxtaposition.[1] This ontological binary portrait reads across multidisciplinary literatures. This study delves into what is here termed "the anthropologized being." Therefore, it becomes clear that we begin with a sketch about a purposeful and derived body of knowledge that endeavors to composite images of a demarcated and fragmented sense of humanity that has had social effects on our civil society and existence.

Anthropology, perceived as a science concerning humanity, helps to manufacture conceptual boundaries not only about the initial and prehistorical human and beast but also about restrictive patterns concerning what I have termed as primary being. Moreover, an inception of being of what traditional Western scholarship has termed as the "other" being are discovered and are noted as existing replicative and insularly worldwide. This Westernized notion of being and non-being identifies and is inclusive of an "othered" African, Native American, Asian, Fanonian's "wretched of the earth," periphery, i.e., primarily trope for the non-white person. Anthropology's roving introspective scientific eye on global cultural customs, behaviors, and patterns has tended towards a useful social cognition and abusive dispersive dissimilitude, which throughout its three hundred years of colonial and disciplinary persistence helped to uphold the present divisive human social formation.

A self-proclaimed science of humanity assists in supplying transpositions of ideas about otherness that inevitably make their way into economic/political/judicial levels. And yet scientific studies still maintain that age-old, European-derived, hierarchical sense of being where profound human relational and imperializing consequences remain injurious. From the start, a rigid and grand scale of ideological certitude persists, as it seemed to have taken the racialist baton from pre-Enlightenment religious institutions.

In this exegesis on a particular knowledge of the past is a review of disciplinary spectra as it pertains to socially destructive and social scientific phrenology-insistence. The generalized concept of an African composite as seen as "Negro," "black," "nonwhite," "other," "primitive," "basic human," "uncivilized human," "prehuman," etc., are also seen as the link between supposedly civilized and bestial forms. It can be seen as structured from the sublimated "basic human" or "near human" at the bottom to the "advanced human" at the top of a hierarchical scale that concerns forms of humanity. Thus, I have construed this structural development as racializational. This is a racialist notion no different from the useful German dichotomy of *naturfolker* (at the bottom) and the *kulterfolker* (at the top), i.e., a binary *existensphilosophie* that has accumulated into the sublime color lining throughout European and American historical time. We are reminded, as Kelly points out on a forward for Robinson's excellent primer entitled *Black Marxism* that it was in the West, hence Europe, and thus not Africa where the "Negro" was first manufactured."[2]

Lofty anthropological scholarship with an indifference to derivation of abusive societal extrapolations has brought on discrete contemporary intersocietal complexities, which especially involve what will be referred to here as *so-called* academic, and yet hidden, and esoteric, presumptive viewing and explication. This disciplinary point of view perpetually works at making peripheral a wrongly described basic African state of being that has traditionally been erroneously regarded as non-being and/or sub-being and therefore minimal historical.

Given all the various manifestations of Western research as witnessed throughout history, Anglo-Saxon derived colonial anthropology has customarily proffered and composed a slanted distant blackness, i.e., an incorporated baseless "otherness" that is fixated at the ends of a devised European scale. This exclusionary Western tendency disallows a persevering African *onta* (i.e., Attic Greek word for "being," read as "existence"). The African *onta* is central to this invective. This extended chronological inquiry is not only critiquing knowledge about human racialized dissimilitude but also the idea of useful human resemblance. The work probes and isolates the key struggle for true meaning of humanity. This interpretive and discerning study presents how notions of prehumanity impede an all-inclusive humanity. The typologies project asocial and unequal human existences.

THE STRUGGLE FOR A STUDY OF HUMANITY

In the 1960s there was a desperate plea from an African American activist intellectual who throughout some very rebellious times in the United States had openly shouted at a hypocritical democratic America where it seemed that a

> [w]hite America will not face the problem of color, the reality of it. The well-intended say: "We're all human, everybody is really decent, and we must forget color." But color cannot be "forgotten" until its weight is recognized and dealt with. White America will not acknowledge that the ways in which this country sees itself are contradicted by being black— and always have been.[3]

The excluded "Colored," i.e., meaning human shades and human tones of black skin, brown skin, red skin, yellow skin, green skin, purple skin, etc., remain in the consciousness of an all-worldwide intellectually derived viewing and i.e. white as non-colored, non-offensive, and non-bestial being that discreetly labels and groups via phenotypic forms. This critique directs its attention to this anthropological and European-originated binary spectrum that affects our human social existence.

What is black and what is white have become traditionalized intellectual perceptions that have been arranged long ago and prompted to support primarily the Linnaeian *Homo Europeaus albus*. The black that does not conceive of a threatening "other" remains extant, but philosophically speaking what one perceives of the outside world only differs by variegated referents. We find the rudiments to physiological differences linked with geographic boundaries only as long as we take a vexatious meta-geographical stance. Marimba Ani elaborates on the process of European incorporation of the outsider and she notes that Western viewing can only look upon African art, for example, in the case of aesthetics— as irrational and amoral.[4]

Throughout American history, white racial postulations were never abandoned, and they have always played a role in decisions that affected the United States and in particular the African American endeavor for full human recognition. In an address given in 1862 to a contingent of African Americans, Lincoln changes his plan for African American colonization from Liberia to Central America due to the economic realities of deporting four million people of African descent back across the Atlantic. Lincoln saw slavery as a moral evil but he also believed that:

> [w]e have between us a broader difference than exist between almost any other two races. Whether it is right or wrong I need not discuss, but this physical difference is a great disadvantage to us both as I think your race suffer very greatly, many of them by living among us, while ours suffer from your presence. In a word we suffer on each side. If this is admitted, it affords a reason at least why we should be separated.[5]

American leadership, an extension of the European sociocultural civilization with its ruling elites and the ideal of a racially similar society, maintained the ideas of difference and justification for not only global partitioning but also believing that social diversity is harmful at any level. Here, it should also be noted that "nineteenth-century anthropologists" influenced Lincoln's attitude on the question of African enslavement, and his concept of race was in keeping with a "reified white superiority."[6] In the United States during the 1960s, contentious, vocal, and self-liberating African Americans sought to excel such human and sociopolitical schematizing distinctions. It is the revelation of the denial of the African (noted as the black) being that has invigorated further striving for civil liberties in modern civilization and that has led many, like Toure in the United States in the 1960s, to present indictments against harmful and divisive Euro-North American and modern reconstructions. The struggle to eradicate "black" and perpetually present blackness as villainous and harmful to a white nurturing United States had long since been an issue.

"MAN" AND ITS GENERALIZED MASCULINITY

Anthropology, a towering and socially unconnected scholarship that produces scientific explications and validity about the natural world and humanity, is draped with a not easily visible pontificating and legitimatizing covering. Anthropological perspectives and Western intellectual perceptions about humanity overall have been notwithstanding a severe hindrance to social harmony. Since its biased inception in the eighteenth century and derivation thereof, anthropology, a study devoted to knowledge of humanity that produces various interpretives (i.e., meanings) of humanity, continues to reinforce the importance of deficient interconnectedness despite working within a now realized and an interminably extant and visibly multiple cultural worlds.

First, what precisely do I mean by anthropology? Simplistically, and etymologically, the word *anthropology* derives from the Greek word ἄνθρωπος (*anthropos*) which comes in two forms: (1) masculine and (2) feminine, and formally translates to "man," as in "man as a whole," and rightly, in the sense of "human beings." Discriminately, and predominately, the Greek stem *anthrop*–has been sublimely considered to solely mean *man*, that is *man* in an all-out masculinized sense, and in the English speaking realm this is primarily due to an Anglo-American precedence for we are reading and interpreting in English. In English, the word "human" itself sublimates that same sense of "man" (i.e., hu-*man*) and so we should reveal that we are still confined to that abominable and yet restrictive, masculinized and hidden intent. The "human" term is Latin derived, *humanus* meaning "human, humane, humankind," it too once implied the class conscious and lofty sense of the German initiated term of *cultured* and to some even "well educated, sophisticated" and, yes, "*bourgeoisie* refined." This sense of "human" worked at an existence separate from the beasts that were supposedly found in nature. Embedded meanings of humanity help to structure the boundary between the uncultured and the cultured, the unhuman and the human. Remember that the hu-*man* being finds that certain kind of *man* remains at the center of meaning.

In 1865, right after the end of the American Civil War, the great Frederick Douglass fought for justified African American human recognition and he put forward the revolutionary idea of self-empowerment and enfranchisement. He battled against American hypocrisy in a piece entitled "What the Black Man Wants."[7] In this instance, Sojourner Truth would clearly attest that "man" actually did mean the masculinized human and that this feminine omission was of course conflictual. Thus, we think of Christ who was a profound *man*, but Sojourner reminds us and reasons that yes, he was a *man* but could only have derived because of a woman.[8] Michele Wallace had understood the significance of holism when within three years' time of joining the Black Panther Party she came to the realization that "the countless speeches that all began with 'the black man…' did not include [her]."[9] Alternatively, take the invincible Assata Shakur who also recognized that her help in what could be described as a contradictory struggle would only make her "moderately liberated," as pretending "doe-eyed" looking women joined in the cause who could not notice that posters of their leaders "conspicuously" excluded women.[10]

The use of man thus restricts race, class, and gender sensibilities and it remains problematic from a capitalistic and a more specific anthropological understanding. With anthropology, specifically we must explicate the term itself. The word anthropology has the suffix "logy" which is commonly used in other words like sociology, psychology, epidemiology, etc. It comes from the Greek word λογος (*logos*), here understood as meaning "study." In Western philosophy the word *logos* takes on various meanings such as "mind, reason, rationale" and so on, but this exegesis refers to it simply in the aspect of "study" as in the study undertaken in a discipline. Hence, generally, the word *anthropology* should literally mean the "study of or about human beings." The centric European *man* standard attempts to relocate a universal, non-gendered, and unbiased being, but it fails since we find that such use only facilitates a sectional term and so non-universal.

For instance, in other European non-English languages, some identifiers also do not relate to this sense of a *universum* or an all-comprising humanity. Take for example the use of the French term *humanité* for "human kind" and or "humanity" as opposed to the term *homme* for the single gender "man" which is quite fair and we can further easily note a slight distinction. Then there is the German *der Mensch*, for "man" and "human being" working in the same fashion as "man" does in English. Yes, there is humanity, *das Menschsein*, and there is the term *Menschlich* as in *die menschliche Rasse*, "the human race." Or better yet, there is the Nazi notion of *die herren Rasse*, i.e., "the master race." Also, take the German philosopher Johann Gottfried von Herder's *Ideen zur Philosophie der Geschichte der Menscheit* (1784–1791), which had been translated and published in 1968 by Frank E. Manuel (a British scholar) as *Reflections on the Philosophy of the History of Mankind*. Here we find once again that centric man that always seems to re-emerge and infer very little of a *universum* theoretical framework.

Nevertheless, we can make out other distinctions between subtle and overt examples, like in German when we find *der Mensch ist ein politishe Wesen*, as in "*man* is a political animal," which alludes to a male overtone. Yet, it is not as strong as *der Mann* as in *ein Mann ein Wort*, "a man's word is his bond," which we can conclude carries the strong masculinist tone that I am addressing here.

This is not a specialized study of the perceptiveness of hidden signs and or the transformational pronunciations of words as per linguistical and Saussurian attributes; rather, this study involves *über*-Saussurian implications and rationalistic expressions that lend themselves to semiotic corollary and psycho-linguistic use of terms and meanings. Being so, this study points to the psycho-signal effects of terms. Making use of the Greek root word σημειον, or "*semion*," meaning "sign or mark" helps to understand "man" in this immediate instance (which also enables the restriction of "female," "proletarian," "black," "race," and/or "nonhuman") either written or interoperated and deduced by writers viewing and anthropologizing beings. This review on "man" markers and or meaning can be seen as proffering indicators of paradigms that are socially affective.[11] It is not just sounds of words that help create images in our minds. I would also assert that a suggestive sign with hidden and subtle meaning interacts between reader and writer. When we read "man" in a literary manner, we find that meaning itself produces a subliminal and affective allusion to a masculine "man," this image remains an indelible mark in our now gendered, racialized, class-organized and conditioned minds, in our now predominately reconditioned, and single-sex rationality. Ultimately, we find acceptance.

Moreover, by this semantic assessment we can understand that even a Greek root like *anthropos* can function as a masculinized text and that inevitably it is fueled by Anglo-American use. We us knowledge that effects our understanding about humans and through a European paradigm we maintain a demarcated boundary where the European male is intersectional and masculinizes and still serves to uphold a narrow Western social tendency. The narrowness plagues our understanding of who we are as humans and helps to impede human interconnectivity. Discretely, the textual use of *man* primarily incited by past and present European writers and thinkers has always meant "this great man," "this colonial and bourgeois man," "this controlling, owning, and ruling man." In addition, we learn from Western ancient philosophy this very same *man* "becomes the measure of all things...," and so too are we mystified into accepting a morphed hierarchal order of things as all the rest and deemed secondary people are continually made peripheral and considered insignificant and nonexistent and kept at a substratum level.

This disciplinary *logos* becomes more inherent of μῦθος (*mythos*) "myth" than the unbiased reason that I am pleading for here in this dialectical contextualization of the many manifestations of this idea of race and demarcated humanity. Unfortunately, for the world as a whole, the European *man* has historically categorized and still categorizes the world from *his own* respective worldview. This particularized "man" although still indefinable or evolving remains centric and maintains a world held by *his own* standpoint. The indivisible, racializing derivative and European-descendent works, views, makes anthropological, and endures and re-creates worlds as they respond and reflect from *him* alone.

The disciplinary endeavor to define humanity in black and white reveals a devised structure. Certain modern translations of ancient writers point out this pervasiveness in defining manliness. Intellectual venues produce models that engage in a comparative elite European-male base, all things of any ancient period and beyond have been preponderantly skewed toward elite European-descendent and supremacist maleness. From the Enlightenment period onwards, we can notably perceive that knowledge about the past, which had been passed down, has been continuously visibly partial.

It is the perceived partialness and the difference that a noun can make (or a pronoun makes in this instance) that brings thoughts about those being objectified. In particular, the European masculinization of a study has remained invariable. It is more than Charles Altieri's inferences about contemporary multicultural warriors at the gates who work out arguments intent on destroying a serviceable past. Altieri states:

> I think we can go a long way toward those arguments if we begin by focusing on the fact that our own capacity to manipulate personal pronouns enables us to experience the "we" simply by reflecting on the versions of "as" that the "I" takes on. Mastery of the grammar of pronouns is inseparable from a rich sense of how the "we" can operate, if only as a sense of our own powers to entertain multiple identifications.[12]

Altieri's concern for how the "we" operates in a universal sense unfortunately fails to wholeheartedly and meta-interpretatively address his "our own powers to entertain multiple identifications." This *own*-ness presents a symptomatic example that works within his critique. Thus, the ruinous ramifications of still yet another Western endeavor to eradicate competing and unentertained identities plague us. From the beginning the European descendent male, "we" has never meant to include the African descendent notion of "we" or, for an extended matter, the bourgeoisie. The "I," the standard tower of centrality, has done more harm by its solitude throughout the ages "as" it sequentially yearns, still awaits, and orders all that exist around it. Certainly, Altieri had to mean more:

> When we turn to the world beyond the subject we find severe limits to that mastery: there are differends that cannot be understood in the speaker's language. But the grasp of such limits requires setting other persons against the "I," and the negotiating of such limits entails the full play of pronominal roles. Even then, however, we encounter the considerable gulf between understanding possible selves and becoming an ethical agent. Knowledge is not action, and the capacity to understand need not be correlated with the will to understand.[13]

The multiple selves are vying for true singularity in a world engulfed by the abyss of differences. Negotiable events accrue as the ideal *modus vivendi* struggled for and found in a conjunctured sameness. Thus, "capacity" and "will" are seen as dichotomous. One may have a strong "will" and a proven agency but lack the "capacity" to be understood; the spirit is outweighed by form. Masculinized "capacity" matters most, but to the "we" that I speak of, the "will" is everything: conscious knowledge and the cognitive metaphysic about obtained *universum* being revealed as empowering and therefore active and activating. In addition, such concerns are passed down and still worked within an imbalanced and perpetual mal-textual that for "us" remains troublesome. This is to say, the African descendent "we" envisioned "as" peripheral form continues to matter less and less "as" the mastery of grammar and the dominancy of a select derived masculinized notion perseveres and still masquerading in falseness.

Yes, we are engaged, i.e., the reader, "you," and the "writer," me, are engaged: the intellectual assumptive positioning that resides hidden behind pronouns interminably interactive. "We" are all locked in an inter-subjective systemic that constrains and appropriately then imagines proper and universal and in a non-abusive sense an insurmountable "we." Sociolinguistic parameters are inherent with partialities and multiple meanings and specific misunderstandings that are at times devastating and exclusive but yet can allow for worldly growth.

For the moment, let us first move to the *Bible* for an *exemplum bonum* of the trans-figurative abusive use of the *anthropos* that the author refers to. Let us review the *Septuagint* Greek where it mentions God's making of *man* (again) in "*his own*" image. One can easily assert that from a Judeo-Christian-Islamic tradition that there are presumptive masculinist notions. One is reminded of what it means to be human as seen in English from the sense of a singly gendered "man." In the Old Testament in the first part of *Genesis 1:26* one can read καὶ ἔιπεν ὁ Θεὸς ποιησαμεν καὶ ἔιπεν ὁ Θεὸς ποιησαμεν ἄνθρωπον κατ᾽εἰκόνα ἡμετέραν καὶ καθ᾽ ὁμοίωσιν·.[14]

And here is my translation, "And God said, Let us make the human being according to our image and likeness." Despite the collectiveness of a jussive and pluralized God with "Let us make," the reader should transliterate and comprehend from the *koine* Greek that there can be either a neutered or masculine humanity, τὸ ἀνθρῴπινον, but unfortunately, many translations have not expressed this.[15] In *Genesis 5:1–2* one finds the second creativity and again the use of the Greek word ἄνθρωπος (*anthropos*) which literally reads, and, again here taken from the *Septuagint*:

> Ἀυτη ἡ Βίβλος γενέσεως ἀνθρῴπων· ἧ ἡμέρα ἐποίησεν ὁ Θεύς τὸν Αδὰμ, κατ᾽ εἰκόνα Θεοῦ ἐποίησεν ἀυτόν· Ἄρσεν καί θῆλυ ἐποίησεν ἀυτούς· καὶ εὐλόγησεν ἀυτούς· καὶ ἐπωνόμασε τὸ ὄνομα ἀυτοῦ Αδὰμ, ἧ ἡμέρα ἐποίησεν ἀυτούς.[16]

Here is an appropriate and connotative translation:

> This is the book of the genesis of humanity; on the day that God made Adam God made him according to the image of God. Male and female God made them and God blessed them and God named him Adam on the day that God made them.

My translation is quite different than what has been included and what I consider to be a male-centered and traditional translation. The following is from the book specifically in marginal format:

> This is the genealogy of men in the day in which God made Adam in the image of God he made him: (2) male and female he made them, and blessed them; and he called his name Adam, in the day in which he made them.[17]

Although some would argue that this is imprecisely interpreted, there is nonetheless a subliminal message being transferred to the gendered audience. We find *anthropos*, or in this instance and in this particular extrapolation partial use of ἀνθρῴπων, "of humans," in genitive plural form and thus as subliminally oblique and slanting to the singly "*of man*." In the original Greek taken from the *Septuagint* one finds talk of male and female (ἄρσεν καί θῆλυ), but when one reads English translations of any contemporary versions, one finds that stress has been placed on maleness because that is what one initially and psychoanalytically in the sense of images thinks when one reads *man* and thus a skewed sense of knowledge (in a biblical setting) is passed down throughout time to a contemporary incorporating audience. The readers become conditioned and exist within what I will regard here as European male derived centrality. It is a repeated socializing process (due to our English and Anglicized interpretive reading) that biblical understandings from the Greek version have been used to support a male solipsism, i.e. that the male self is sufficiently valid to represent all of humanity.

Now from a potent feminist and masculinized-doddering stance, how can biblical knowledge instruct women to read and write and conceptualize? How intellectually useful can this all-viewing help? Can they design a self-esteemed craft using these literary, marbleized, and partisan traditions that have replicated dominancy? How can intellectualized femininity work through creatively unfettered and unbiased by such inappropriate, universalized, masculinized notions? They are bombarded with uni-gendered and unicultural interpretations. The anti-text affects the non-European-derived reader. The old literary text of a time long gone is a foreign past. Forrester sorrowfully writes, "We don't know what women's vision is. What do women's eyes see? How do they carve, invent, and decipher the world? I don't know. I know my own vision, the vision of one woman, but the world seen through the eyes of others? I only know what men's eyes see."[18] The feminine is inherently a part of the negation that I speak of here for it will be observed that the feminine is intellectually seen as receding into suspended identities and is subsumed into the virtual. The same virtual that affects those deemed nonwhite.

In another instance from early Greek philosophy, the term *anthropos* again subliminally loses the sense of the *universum* being and here again the reader will find more abusive use of *man*. Aristotle, one of the Greek Parthenon gods of Western philosophy, in *Physis* reasons through forms or rather the binary nature of things, i.e., the principles of the appearance of coming into being from what is and from what is not. Aristotle uses *anthropos* in various sections, but here in the beginning of his book the form of natural beings is discussed. In *Book I vii 190a 5–14* Aristotle uses the term *anthropos* (ἄνθρωπος) and he goes to state:

> Τούτων δὲ τὸ μὲν οὐ μόνον λέγεται τὸδε γίγνεσθαι ἀλλὰ καὶ ἐκ τοῦδε ῾(ὃιον ἐκ μὴ μουσικοῦ μουσικός)· Τὸ δ᾽ οὐ λέγεται ἐπὶ πάντων οὐ γὰρ ἐξ ἀνθρῴπου ἐγένετο μουσικός, ἀλλ᾽ ἄνθρωπος ἐγένετο μουσικός· Των δὲ γίνομένων ώς τὰ άμλᾶ λέγομεν γίγνεσθαι, τὸ μὲν ὑπομένον γίγνεται τὸ δ᾽ όιχ ὑπομενον· ό μὲν γὰρ ἄνθρωπος ὑπομένει μουσικός γινόμενος ἄνθρωπος καὶ ἔστι, τὸ δε μὴ μουσικός καὶ τὸ ἄμουσον οὔτε άπλω οὔτε συντιθέμενον ὑπομένει.[19]

Again, I provide the following translation as others continue within a Europeanizing centrality:

> From this, we can say that not only is it possible that something becomes something, but also that something becomes something out of something else (like an uncultivated person becoming *cultivated*). But we cannot say this of all things, for from just being a human being the person does not become cultivated, but as a human being the person can become cultivated.
> And knowing this, as we say both become something, the cultivated person and the not cultivated person become something, for it is known that the cultivated human being becomes cultivated and is cultivated, but the uncultivated or non-cultivated is either both or combined.

In this excerpt, Aristotle (like the many pre-Socratic and ancient Egyptian-trained philosophers that came before him and many Western thinkers that came after him) engages in the dialectical grand debate between what is the underlying substance or form that takes greater precedence, nature or nurture. It is a competitive duality, i.e., the causality of being and nonbeing that has, so it seems, plagued so many thinkers in the West and in particular for this review Western antiquity.

In the selected example we find the use of the Greek term *anthropos* which should correctly be directed to all humanity, but instead as in other English translations, unfortunately remains latently biased throughout the ages. In fact, it continues onward as a harmful semiotic referent that one could further assert has had various socializing effects. We must comprehend this as literature that has helped to instill gendered and racial dominance.

For instance, when we read a later translation, specifically Waterfield's modern translation, we find a more creative disguising with its superb implementation of substituting *man* for *person* and neutering many things, but we still have "...a person persists –*he* is still a person when *he* has become educated... [Italics mine]."[20] And then there is Blackwell who works on a commentary by the Western Aquinas and who makes use of Aquinas's analogy of the "musical man."[21] It is Ioanne Baptista Camotio who fittingly makes comparative use of the Greek *anthropos* with the Latin *Homo* and this is so only because it is exclusively in the scholarly Latin language of the times which was written in 1554 A.D.[22] Fortunately enough, here in this presentation we are made aware of the European-male traditionalized usage of the term *anthropos* and this enquiry will refer to the proper pretransliterative intent and meaning, that is, its reference to all of humanity, both genders and all peoples that make up the human species, i.e., the actual sense of *anthropos-logos* and not the still European and male traditionalized anthropology that others from a solely gendered-centric perspective.

DE-ANTHROPOLOGIZING

Let us move beyond classical meta-symbolism with their transliterations and their harmful presumptions and turn to the need for an ameliorative definition for anthropology. Anthropology can be understood as representing a "hybrid discipline uniting at least two distinct scholarly traditions: the natural historical and the social theoretical (with input as well from various lines of humanistic inquiry)."[23] Anthropology today should concern itself with the scientific study of the origin of humanity, and the physical, behavioral, social and cultural development of human beings. Anthropology as a field of study has explained many phenomena and constructed many theoretical perceptions about a specific humanity's existence both past and present.

In this analysis, the anthropological field of study, as a whole, should regard a multi and at all times sub-disciplinary field of knowledge that must regard fair actualities that exist about all of humanity and not just from a predominating white with an ancillary black base where densely white researchers work on symbolized black specimens. The stifling ethnicized and encumbering othering practices maintain a perpetual exclusivity. Anthropology should uphold perceptions on balanced origins of humanity that render the true beginnings of a worldwide social and *pan to anthropinon* (humanity) and that additionally does not furnish dominant/sub-servant and unfair social implications to the cognizant and inductive modern intellectual world.

In order to simplify this socio-intellectual analysis on what will be posited as profoundly repercussive knowledge and reproductive scholarly information about humanity, this study portends that a biased anthropology includes various and sometimes almost autonomous sub-disciplinary lines of study. Since the work submitted here almost entirely concerns itself with archaeologic interpretations about prehuman origins or rather generalized discernments on origins of humanity. It should be noted that this evaluation delves into paleo-anthropological interpretations of what it means to tend towards humanity as has been hypothesized by an anthropology that customarily still churns out devised paleo-human theorizations and that assiduously makes partial rather than impartial use of archaeological remains from certain prehistoric periods.

Anthropology depends upon and interprets the archaeological evidence and anthropology creates useful and abusive paleo-anthropological explanations that redevelop within a more self-perceived, i.e. more somewhat scholarly and regressive, self-informed, self-validated, and renewed and still sole-white anthropologized postmodernity. In particular physical anthropology (just as in the color-lines of Selma, Alabama in 1954, the apartheid beaches of Soweto, South Africa in 1985, or the present sections of Brooklyn, New York) creates greater divisiveness. Thus, overbearingly it can be viewed as a white academic edifice that still fertilizes false ideas about the expansive "nonwhite" world, i.e., a multiculturalistic world that is processed through a white-male conducive vision. It is a restrictive academic fellowship that is respective of a preselected hu(man) derivation that contractively remains contingent upon the key sub-disciplinary white-utilitarian and white-buttressing archaeology.

Long ago, anthropology, initially meant the early dated sub-disciplines of (1) archaeology (now more scientific), (2) ethnology (now regarded as cultural/social or behavioral anthropology), and (3) physical anthropology (formerly known back in the late 1800s and early 1900s as somatology because it dealt with anatomy, and hence its use of the Greek neuter root to σωμα, σώματος (*somatos*) which literally translates as "body [more dead than alive] of human being (or beast"). In order to re-contextualize anthropology this enquiry plainly indicates that anthropology has grown more specialized and has reinvigorated itself with more precise identifications and more detailed labels and, in particular, more skewed use and abuse from such sub-field categorizations as primatological, molecular and evolutionary which add intra-disciplinary specificity. In other words, the field has become more sophisticated in its propagation of racist notions of what it means to be human.

This deconstruction must identify traditional anthropology as continuing through an imperial pattern and we attend to the qualms of the *contrapposto* Black anthropology for anthropology as whole remains conflicted. Back in 1980, a journal entitled *The Black Scholar: Journal of Black Studies and Research* presented a two part series entitled "Black Anthropology," and in the very beginning of this two part series we are informed that the two imposing journal issues will be entirely devoted to

> the cultural anthropology of African and Afro-American people. It is also the first collection of works by Afro-American anthropologists. However, the importance of this publication must rest on more than the fact that it exists for the first time. It should be judged by the extent to which it contributes to ongoing efforts to sever anthropology's intimate associations with colonialism, imperialism and racism. Anthropology was born during the 18th century, but it grew up precisely during the period of imperialist penetration of the cultures of people of color in Africa, Asia, and the Americas. Thus anthropology served the needs of imperialist and colonialist powers to know more about the people they subjugated … the better to rule them.[24]

Back in 1980, Johnetta B. Cole and Sheila S. Walker edited and struggled to make a point clear within a proper academic *discipline*. They fought as educationally empowered and politically conscious African American scholars (disciplinary vindicationist) against what could be called a destructive traditional anthropology.

The renowned American intellectual St. Clair Drake sets the first issue off with historical information about the liberal American struggles against "Establishment anthropologists"[25] There were political battles as Ashley Montagu fought against the crafty Harvard-based work of Carleton Coon. Drake points to what he calls "the racial vindication," otherwise known as the vindicationists like Franz Boas and W.E.B. Du Bois who made heroic counter-offensives against what I would call the ruinous underhanded workings of early anthropology. Drake protested against the use of a maligning and supposed scientific authority that validated early twentieth century human cephalic indices. Drake, a valiant critiquing savant, informs us about W.E.B. Du Bois' fight against the anthropological ruminations of black civilizational and degenerate propaganda that was purportedly due to scientifically induced concepts of "Mongrelization" attached with the idea of an unfettered and savage blackness.[26]

There can be no doubting that traditional anthropology has quite adeptly worked under the guise of "scientific authority" to help sustain a human social cognitive condition. One wonders why anthropology did not fall in on itself considering all the fallacious and creative rubbish that helped propel an unbalanced human world. In the same issue, there was also Whitehead who is sentimentally troubled and displays concern about the biasness that is a "major barrier to establishing our discipline as an objective science."[27] And thus, presently twenty-three years later can we say that anthropology has progressed and that those qualms uttered in those two 1980 issues of *The Black Scholar* have been resolved. Not in the least. There was an awry viewing by traditional anthropology as strictly in accordance with Western tradition and that ingeniously continued to negate any non-European entity. The study of *anthropos* should work within a better and more useful *pan to anthropinon* that is all enveloping and inclusive of non-European aspects that otherwise maintain rightful and equal space.

Moreover, certain paleoprimatological research should not resolutely explain away variant perceptions; early twentieth century Western scientific intelligentsia intent on validating superiority produced anthropometric interpretation on anatomical remains which became quite useful to support skewed and racializing comparative assessments. Again, there is a need for better developed and more unconcocted study of *anthropos* as advocated long ago by the foremost Haitian anthropologist Antenor Firmin who had argued against the misuse of anthropology.[28] Thus, blackness as understood by anthropology and as pertaining to the concept and categorization of being not white peoples, nations, and ethnicities was solely formulated as a means of maintaining control. It was controlled by the preconceived, traditionalized and established Western or European aesthetic or white ideal. Allow me to also remind us that many ancient peoples such as those residing in Kush, Kemet, and Keftiu, were explained away as being white Hamites (read Europeanized), and consequently, it remained historical and significant; racializing categories serve solely one ulterior purpose: European historic dominance.

This exegesis argues that the development of a conceptualized white ideal standard stemmed academically from an anthropology that worked at creating dividing lines with European descendants at the top and African descendants at the bottom in a chain of human entities which not only explained how humanity or prehumanity came to be but also how traditionalized anthropology accumulated a body of knowledge and acquired information and made analyses (both indiscreetly and discreetly) with described African physiognomy, behavior and fossils. Scholarly perceptions of Indo-European genealogy represent rediscovered "racialized" polarities and by the1850s represented a self-validated usefulness with Western diacritical and reified "nonwhite" and marked "true Negro" entities.

This work describes that beginning with the eighteenth century European and American ethnological analyses and descriptions of a black African, by Western thought, in particular, solidified and aggrandized an African burdensome existentialism that still remains throughout what can now be referred to as (post) but improvised-colonial-istic American era. Divided here into chapters is the first part of an extensive presentation that exposes perceptions. In the chapters that follow the reader will survey other areas of study such as taxonomy, geology, paleontology and molecular as well as paleo-anatomical biology. Such studies will be reviewed in order to draw a multidisciplinary portrait of a discipline overall. A discipline that still works at defining and elucidating a certain kind of humanity and that still continues to this day to negate through the use of an insurmountable European and American bearing stances. At times it works through skewed extemporizing notions of humanity that can never be universal.

Historically speaking, anthropology has primarily worked at subjugating what has been construed as "black" cultures whether in present times or in past times in what erroneously has been initially perceived as unhistorical. Traditionally, studies on humanity have wrongly imposed and universalized realms that have caused more harm than good. The study of *pan to anthropinon* works not only to properly work through an all-inclusive acquiring body of knowledge where e.g. the African perspective also maintains its significant space but also it works at instilling a better sense of the universal being for building socially harmonious future civilizations, societies, and of course for a purely multiple and all-encompassing perpetuity.

NOTES

1. Please note that Black, in this instance, has been traditionally lumped and signified in the guise of non-whiteness and the conceptionalization of whiteness has traditionally also

included other groups of people see Graves, p. 4–5 on whiteness and its "Anglo-Saxon and Teutonic' superiority paradigm."

2. Robin D. G. Kelly's foreword sums up Robinson's rationalization for beginning his work with feudalistic Europe, p. xiii.

3. Carmichael (Kwame Toure) p. 245.

4. p. 204.

5. Excerpt from Moses, p. 210 see also p. 28 and p. 209 for comments on Lincoln's antislavery position.

6. See Graves on Lincoln and the sciences rise to establishing validity for human variation p. 55, see also 56 on the topic of "humanness of the Negro" and its incompatibility with chattel enslavement.

7. See Marable et al, p. 125–131.

8. Marable, et al, p. 68.

9. Marable et al, p. 520.

10. Marable et al, p. 534.

11. Saussure p. 16.

12. P. 316.

13. *Ibid.*

14. See Brenton p. 2.

15. See the various *Bible* versions: New International Version, New Revised Standard Version, and King James's Version.

16. See Brenton p. 6.

17. *Ibid.*

18. P. 56–57.

19. The author extrapolated the Greek from *Loeb Class. Ser.*, see Goold (ed.) p. 72. The author also supplies his own translation as the translation work of Wicksteed, who died before publication back in 1929, maintains male-centricism.

20. See Aristotle translated by Waterfield, p. 25.

21. See Thomas translated by Blackwell p. 49.

22. See Pselli *Primus Bii 30–40* beginning with *Genitarvm.*

23. Bynum *et al. Dictionary of the History of Science*, p.19.

24. Excerpted from front cover page of Part I, see Cole.

25. See Drake, p. 2.

26. *Ibid.*, p.10.

27. See Whitehead, p.86.

28. See Antenor Firmin (1885) who had been ignored for over one hundred years and who has resurfaced thanks to some conscious African-American scholars who understand the imperative need to battle white anthropology. Firmin's book long ago critiqued white anthropology, it was a book primarily written as a response to Gobineau's intensely racist anthropological work that had been written back in 1853 through 1855. Firmin fought back in 1885 and it seems that even after almost one hundred years black anthropologists such as the ones mentioned above from the issues in 1980 of *Black Scholar* display that a strain persists. The black struggle against Western thought began years ago and still remains silenced and negated. On a contemporary reporting see Dobhartz and see Hage (see particularly the reasons for resurgence of belief structures of White "purity" that Hage points to in his analysis on Australian White and non-White present-day clashes).

Chapter One

The Cosmic Origin

STELLAR ORIGINS

In our present hastening and forever increasing "inter(net)ed" times, we have long come to appreciate the comforts that science brings to humanity, and we easily comprehend that being scientific means working within the ideal of a better system, i.e. a more useful and far reaching use of acquired knowledge. We believe in the goodness of science and we respect the function and process of science as it endeavors to reveal not only the workings in obtainable *explananda* but also the origins of nature overall. Science has answered many questions and also rationalizes human existence. Science explains that our warming sun propels life on earth.

It is a scientific fact that humanity lives in an aged earth that is geologically estimated at being 4.8 billion years old. Science has also formulated the idea that humanity has transformed into who we now are in what would be considered a relatively minuscule period of spatial and continual time. In a very short period of time compared to our earth's existence it seems that humanity has been formed through existential and morphological processual occurrences that have led to the present and extraordinary result of contemplative human beings. It is believed that we will continue to transform as the universe, i.e. the largest possible volume of space together with all its matter, proceeds to radiate and extend outward without limit to an unfathomable fourteen billion light years far in every direction.[1]

Incessantly, universal changes seem inevitable given all the time and space at hand and if we defend the origins of organisms and entity transformations, then we must equally come to understand that our stupendous sun also has had an origin and thus was born in a gaseous cloud around about almost five billion years ago. Subsequently, our sun will also one day come to extinguish as similarly as what astronomy has discerned from all the other ever increasing stellar appearances and disappearances that have been observed by the ever more powerful and gigantically enhanced telescopes.

In our scientific understanding of the origin of our sun we must here also indicate that our life sustaining sun with all its heat and bursting intensity is part of an enormous family of other suns, i.e., our sun is an astonishing speck which is an integral part of thousands upon thousands of sun-like stars that make up our galaxy, i.e. called the Milky Way. It has been estimated that galaxies and galaxies exist in this universe and like the endless stars that we see in a clear night sky they are numerous and insurmountable. They can be described as being as limitless as the small grains of sand on a beach; they are perceived as being unfathomably endless.

We exist within a great family of stars which scientifically is believed to have been born at some fixed past moment. The Great Big Bang can still be considered a somewhat protean conception that exists in a somewhat unrealizable point in time. Many scientific estimates and calculations have been made by generations of astronomists, philosophers and mathematicians alike and when we ponder about the ungraspable beginnings: the universe, galaxy, sun, earth, and humanity, we surmise from modern science that certain beginnings seem still at times unobtainable, incomprehensible, and yet explicable.

FAMILIAL ANCESTRIES

When precisely did the first prime human existence occur? Here creationism and evolutionism expend a great deal of time and trouble in debate. The origin of all origins perhaps remains multiple. A nonreligious answer of the ultimate life-question, for some, remains faithfully solvable and spiritually acceptable, and yet for others, there are only perpetual (re)formulated hypothesizations and (re)newed theorizations that almost always inevitably become, in a Popper-ian sense, refutable. There can be no doubt that the origin of humanity is still a very intense topic.

The exact point in time of when demarcated humanity begins remains a conundrum. Many have wondered how far back scientists can really go consistently in tracing our human family tree to its originating moment in respect to the expansive time and spatial continuum. Some have considered maternal mitochondrial DNA to be, in a metaphorical sense, disclosing and decisive recorded data of our human past, but we must bear in mind that despite all the advanced technology at hand, genetic maps are still too imprecise and speculative to fundamentally point out and display definitive trace nodes of past permutationalized human distinctions. Nonetheless, geneticists have become bio-internal archaeologists as they peer ever so deeply into a grandiose mapped-out genome that will require more refined markers and better identified and more common protein shapes as they further elongate and diachronologize the permutated traces of connective life.[2]

Presently, working within a historical local level we can self-reflect and turn to our own personal family tree and think, how far, really, within our own personal families can the earliest time of familial existence be found. What is the earliest point of time, or rather, how far back can any present-day human draw connected genealogical and generational lines to? How far back can we personally within our own families really go? Undoubtedly, it seems that we cannot go too far back. Most average families worldwide can really only go as far back as to their great-great grandparents, i.e. before various propensities of speculation and creativity begin to increase.

On a religious spectrum, there is of course the biblically recorded grand line of descendants in *Genesis* that speak of and describe linked individuals, tribes and overall ideal human familial unity. And then there is the English monarchy that maintains a lineage that covers twelve centuries and thirty-eight generations of familial connectivity.[3] There is also the lineage of the Australian convicts, which comes from *Charles Bateson's Convict Ships* (found in the Library of Australian History which is also out of print) where Bateson states that 160, or rather a total of 151 convicts were sent to Australia. It is believed that most were from the British Isles and some from British colonies.[4] The British government first sent convicts to New South Wales, Australia in 1788 after the American Revolution, and it is believed that many names and genealogical traces can be made by descendants of Australian families. Also in the recent past, there are church registers that have gone as far back as the seventeenth century when registers were first introduced and even perhaps some aristocratic clans can also slightly go further back.[5] Overall, such genealogical and familial designations can be considered somewhat still elided and partially self-derived for the intent purposes of establishing ruling cultural heritages and monarchic bloodline recognitions.

Moreover, take as another example of human descendant creativities the Icelandic company Decode Genetics which is led by the CEO and President named Kari Stefansson who is from Iceland and who is also a Harvard trained scientist. Presently the company is working on linking DNA health records with genealogical database charts of families that have been traced back to the original Vikings.[6] One must note that there must be some fictionalizing; the author contends that with any tracing back there will almost always be room for error. The author further asserts that what is truth and what will be truth as time continues evolves and re-evolves and will come to produce established lines of descent. It seems that this special unique island that is comprised of a homogeneous nation of people where their genetic code has now been *scientifically* led back to the original Vikings has both an Icelandic government and a working science joined at the hip to work on further devising connectivity. Iceland has been regarded as a closed population and what I fear most of all is not a concern for the breaches of privacy that are certainly forthcoming in an Orwellian prophetic sense, but what I fear most of all is the heritage affects that data is causing as scientifically guided and approved programs continue to perturb humanity.

It seems that creating human traces has become an essential part of our social existence. According to two Italian anthropologists Piero and Alberto Angela it is *scientifically* proven that humanity can go back about 40, 000 centuries (or better yet four million years ago).[7] Comparatively speaking, along with the short familial and ancestral tracings, we also find shortcomings in what would be perceived as assertions about connectivity from a definitive point in time and from fossilized anthropoidal transformations. We still cannot thoroughly prove categorical and explicit lines to such a prehistoric past even through the use of the superb and technologically advanced analysis of all the discovered, identified, and supposed anthropoid forms. Thus, we are left always theorizing about our human past and we are always endeavoring to (re)discover and (re)present a further extended, connected and substantiated human ancestry.[8] When we intellectualize and reach back to the now somewhat more quantifiable and decipherable prehistoric past we still engage in the interminable endeavor of (re)creatively looking backwards and this task has always entailed troubling missing pieces that still impede solving the mystery of what I will call the *stand-all-single* proof of an ultimate origin of archetypal humanity.

It seems that designed and elaborately engineered explanations about humanity's derivation have almost always required fill-ins and sublime interpretative insertions. Consequentially, almost always we will find hermeneutic immersions that bind us to elaborately legitimatized and scientifically constructed hypotheses that I will call "modern day" mythologies about a select prehistoric ancestry. Despite all the fortunately discovered and meticulously analyzed fossils of teeth, bones, and skulls, we will never come to map out quite entirely humanity's precise morphological passage throughout prehistoric time. We can only continue to idealize *via* a science that most times excludes religion in its exegesis and a science that also comes to know in a presumptive pattern what it explains to *rationally* come before.

BLACK IMPLICATION OF UN-DEVOIDABLE HOLES

Perhaps what really is needed is the scientific creation of a time-traveling device that will enable us to go back and experience the prehistoric past. Perhaps what we need is some miraculous scientific feat of time travel where we would be allowed to conduct an observational survey of a time period long since passed. Retrogressively, it would have to reach back in time crossing through hyperspace, and achieving an astounding deed in the fourth dimension, movement from an optimum point X to a disclosable point Y perhaps respectively faring through what science has called the Einstein-Rosen Bridge.[9] And thus, our hurling device must cruise into a parallel universe, but it must somehow veer and tend to be angulated to land backward in time instead of forward, i.e., imaginatively spanning two universes to some designated point in the past. We must be reminded that such an opportunity still remains scientifically yet unobtainable. The problem stems with trying to cross a bridge without being crushed due to what is called singularity because what are said to surround such a bridge are menacing black holes.

Black holes are regions in spacetime where the gravitational field is so powerful that light cannot even pass through it. The term was first presented by an American Princeton physicist, John Archibald Wheeler, who back in December 29th, 1967 first publicly uttered and coined the term in an after-dinner talk during a meeting of the American Association for the Advancement of Science in New York.[10] The pernicious and combined term of "black" with "holes" sensationalizes various images and gathers much hype. Again, it is the tone of "black" that has made all the difference in the world. It is black holes not worm holes or white dwarfs, but black gravity and depravity that cause a populace to listen. As scientific tradition would have it, it is the blackness that stigmatizes holes into the realm of an ominous mysticism; it is the sense of a wide expansive void of an inescapable blackness that envelopes and destroys. It is the incredibility of "black" holes and such black negative things that leads us to always remain fearful of universal spacetime.

It seems that what science fears most is the self-(re)created and self-(re)envisioned blackness in the white mind and transposed out there into space into the holes that cause gravitational collapses and into the holes that severely apply quantum mechanics. Science works hard at recreating and externalizing our conditioned black intimidation. And thus, I would prefer the pre-late 1960s (before John Archibald Wheeler) specialist usage term of "frozen" or "collapsed stars." [11] Or even better yet why not use what I would like to generally call "space holes" than the connotative use of black holes. Black holes signify an inherent blackness that leads even science fiction writer to work on demystifying it and white-inducing it with ideas about "Angelmasses."[12] It is the heaven-sent angelmass that works within an inherent vile blackness that makes for yet another deprecatory trope explanation of black roots.

To travel through time and to bypass what I would rather not call black holes but space holes of noontime is the interminable pursuit of science. As science continues to quest, perhaps one day it will be proven that black holes may not even be black after all but instead are found to be blank since it may be revealed that as nothing passes and we are reduced to the end of time we irreversibly arrive at nothingness and nonbeing. We arrive at insubstantiality, which leads us to reason that nothingness cannot possibly have color. Nonetheless, mass is drawn in to such a described place with the kind of powerful gravity that ordinarily crushes all things out of existence and into oneness, in a frightening singularity. And yet, we must safely pass through a bridge that connects universes if we can comprehend such matters (see Figure 1.1). We leap, and, omitting the dangers of singularity, we pass between two space holes' surface boundary of what is called the event horizon in order to make it to the other side. And through chance we may not wind up at time-forward, but at the more inconceivable time-backward. And it is this yet to be seen scientific passage and through this temporal exploration without any blundering paradoxes that we encounter a time once passed.

Overall, after we have found a way to time travel back into various geographically specific and prehistoric localities we could take snapshots of

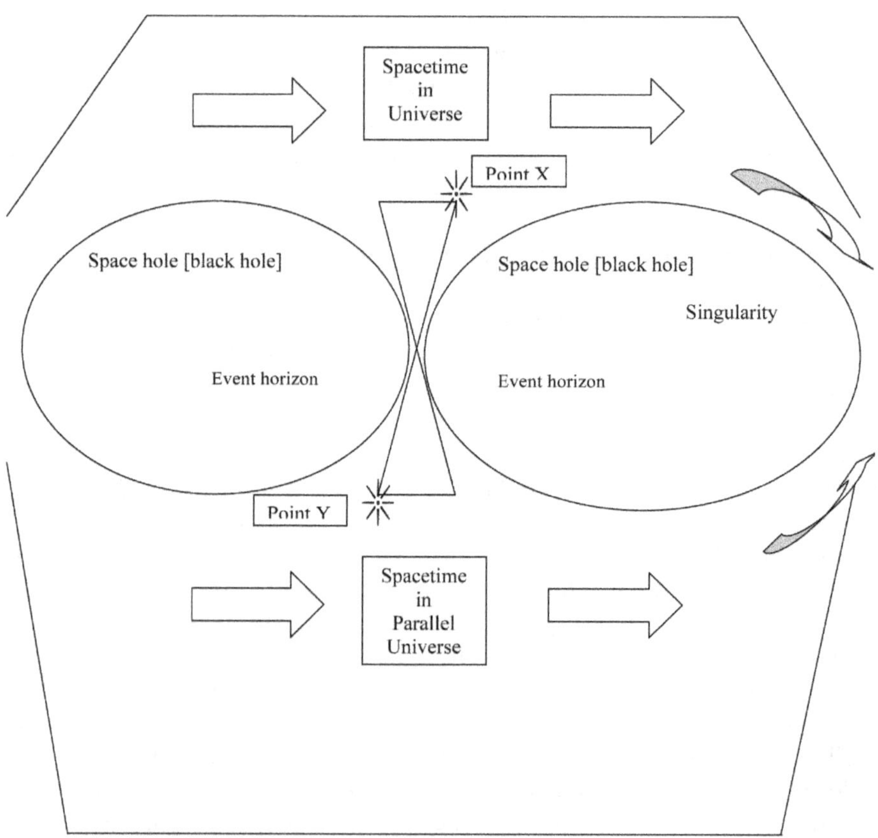

Figure 1.1. Hypothetical Time Travel. This depiction was created by the author.

previous life forms in their actual existence. And even more imaginative, we could fast forward to several geologic events and properly assess how prehuman to human transformations actually precipitated. Along the way we could also take bio-physiological measurements of the encountered fauna and the many passed extinctions and speciations of the many multiple entities especially paying particular attention to what I call transitory proto-apes that inevitably sort of moved on up, evolutionarily, to the next transitory protohuman life forms. Perhaps, then, via a time-traveled voyage, we finally will obtain the truth about what went on. A nonvirtual time-traveled and conscious reliving of the past would definitively solve the interminably unanswerable questions about who we really are and how truly was it that we came to be.

NOTES

1. See Dixon who presents a frightful future to come as time almost endlessly continues and humanity persists, and where we find a progressive gray (neither black nor white, or perhaps an entity composite of a literal black-white combination thereof). Futuristic human forms are depicted; especially interesting is Jimez Smoot's descendant 5 million years from now, p. 121.
2. See Wade's *New York Times*' article, pp. F1 and F7, on news about DNA data (particularly Y chromosome analyzations) used to map out Jewish roots and to help reconstruct ideas about how the diaspora grew.
3. See Hilliam's appendix, a lineage chart that stems from Egbert to Elizabeth II.
4. See www.ancestry.com where Ancestry Plus is an online genealogy library where a database has been compiled with more than 48,000 names of convicts sent to Australia between 1788 and 1868.
5. See www.trentvalleyarchives.com where a master name database that began 26 years ago can be found and where family genealogies of founding families of five counties in Canada are maintained. There is also a claim of descendants from the nine ships of the 1825 Peter Robinson Irish Emigration.
6. See Lyall's *New York Times* article.
7. p. 7.
8. See wireless communication to *The New York Times* dated January 12, 1929 article titled "Skeleton called that of earliest modern man is dug up in Kenya and removed intact." See seventy years later, Haile-Selassie (2001) who asserts human origins at 6 million years ago and this is attested to from the latest bones discovered in Afar, Ethiopia, and this find also adds an additional 2 million years to hominid existence. Also see Lemonick for a *Time Magazine* article in July 2001 on earliest point of humanity dated at 6 million years ago because of the same recent Ethiopian find.
9. See Macvey pp. 120-123.
10. See Israel p. 88.
11. See Frolov *et al.* p. 4.
12. See the science fiction novel entitled *Angelmass* by Zahn.

Chapter Two

Primal Connectivity

A UTILE PRIMATIAL TRIUMVIRATE

It is a believed scientific fact that we resemble anatomically and genetically apes more than any other species in the world. It is because of this factual belief that postDarwinian anthropologists reconstructively study the primate evolutionary process in order to notate cladistically physiological derivations that led to our modern human origins. We are almost identical, genetically speaking of course, with the gorillas and most of all chimpanzees. We have even been viewed as the third chimpanzee next to the pygmy chimp of Zaire and beside the chimp of the rest of tropical Africa.[1]

Strangely enough, we are related, and it is because of this ape-human theoretical bridge that scientists have come to search deep into the earth's ground in pocketed bone preserving dry localities in order to recover prehistoric pithecines and supposed archaic human forms. All the endless pieces of discovered bones have created a taphonomy that has helped to make up the many identified and syncopated forms that in particular physical anthropology has placed in between to reassemble a transformed and sequential pattern of a gradually developing humanity. All the minutiae of detail and description from a small deciduous tooth to a chapped femur have assisted in defining transformational and morphological physiological trajectories that stem to humanity's beast-like origination.

Established conceptualizations about stages of prehuman to human development, from (1) preprimate (or squirrel-like tree shrews) to (2) proto-pithecines (or chimpanzee-like) to (3) pithecanthropines (or enlarged chimpanzee-like) to (4) Neanderthal (or weighty hairless gorilla-like) and to (5) modern humanity, didn't really occur until around the turn of the twentieth century. It was within the beginning of the twentieth century, by 1906, that a German anatomist from Strasbourg, named Gustav Schwalbe set a paradigm of progression and began the stages. Schwalbe initially presented the last three mentioned stages: in particular (3) pithecanthropine (4) Neanderthal and (5) modern humans.[2] Further hypothesizations concerning human transformation become a passed on scientific tradition and in a sense a triumvirate of sub groups within the Primate Order had been established and for a time has been perpetuated.

The last three stages and here I will include as well as the first two, i.e. all five can also be construed as separate, major and distinct characteristic forms that exist without any definitive or discovered evidence of what may fall under punctualistic and or gradualistic intermediate types. We have not found what could be structured as humanoidal temporal links with quasi or transitional physical features, such as the proof positive and archaeological discovery of an enlarged modern brain with ape like prognathicism, or for that matter, a modern cranium with apelike skeletal features, or even a supposed and more enlarged encephalizational level with a parabolic dental shaped mouth. None of these described plausibly in-flux types of temporal intermediaries between stages have been evidentiary and found, and it can be contended, "not as of yet."

A SYLLOGISTIC APPLICATION

After Darwin's theory had presented the belief that a transformational mix of ape-to-human form was to be expected, beginning midway through the nineteenth century the earliest forms of prehumanity were heavily sought after. Through more systematic archaeological excavations there was a scientific sentiment that proof would inevitably be found. A modern Western concept of finding a link between humanity and the beast was a very important maintained presumption in the early part of the twentieth century as well. It is a science that unadmittedly refrains from accepting its dark roots. It is a Westernism that would rather have human origins in Europe, Asia, Australia, or America than in Africa, it is a science forever endeavoring in self-denial.[3]

Let us philosophize for the moment about the theoretical mechanization of conceptualizations about links or ape-human connectivity and let us delve into the scientific inference that became quite useful in creating an entire academic industry in particular, behavioral, physical, and evolutionary anthropology.

An *a priori* simplistic assumption made from the fossil record had been that prehumanity to humanity went through a string of preliminary forms that moved forward from a point A to point B and then to point C and so on and so on, etc. etc. etc. Thus it became the assumption that hominoid predevelopment must have passed through a certain type of mixed form, a point B which resides between an A and a C. Archaeologically, links were logically needed in order to sustain a credible scientific notion. Any kind of link was required in order to support perceptions of transformation from pre-hominids to hominids and from hominids to presently formed humans. Humanity's prehistoric past and its early beginnings could be construed as provable, and thus a belief that underneath the ground lurked humanity's primordial ancestry was held by a community of Western scientific thinkers. Yet as time moved on and passed up through the twentieth century, the point B specimen had remained an unsolvable mystery. What was needed was a form or a point B that would encapsulate some percentage of prehominid and some percentage of prehumanity, or better yet, some percentage of prehumanity and some percentage of humanity.

The need to find the missing link had been so intense and permeating by the beginning of the twentieth century that a group of British scholars initially accepted and spent some time grappling with the reconstruction of a self-proclaimed link, an exact point B type specimen. In fact, so intense was the presumption to find the "half-man and half-ape" form that Western science ideally prevailed and hence, in a European backyard, a discovery was proclaimed. The astounding discovery was *Eoanthropus dawsoni*, Piltdown Man, a reconstruction of a cranium that encapsulated somewhat too perfectly the fusion between humanity and ape.[4]

When we philosophize on a topic such as the prehuman-to-human linkage we come to discussions about continuity, which is to say in a sense controversial human continuity amidst the "creationism-evolutionism" philosophical polar extremes. Let us here in this segment, solely for now, work within the secular position. In the secular viewpoint we can look at the presented theorizations on links from an empiricist or a rationalist perspective. Some have argued that a true empiricist would always come to deny and find disdain in an *a priori* based conclusion. The empirical stance would not tolerate creative rationalizations, if we do not find or (for exploratory purposes) do not have in our hands factual proof of a link, a point B form of development, then there never was one.

On the other hand there is the rationalist who would uphold an opposing idea about links, and present deductively that sequential causality can however exist from a point A form of development to a point C, via a logical point B, the considered presumptive causality matters a great deal because from it evidently we have arrived at both a point A and a point C, two items that can be noted as once existing. We have a point A and we have a point C and the two have appeared with various consequential physical similarities (see Figure 2.1). We have two forms that can be compared. Links reasonably can be believed to exist for if they can be plausibly and rationally be deduced from a progressive homology then some kind of logic merits their assessed interconnected existence.

Causality becomes a conceptualized necessity that involves the creative appearance of (a link) a point B, for realistically the rationalist will point out that it is noted that humanity cannot possibly leap frog from a point A, a lesser form of development, to a point C logically (abiding by natural law) to an advanced entity. Saltationist *ad absurdum* argumentation has been ridiculed. A saltatorial attitude counter-poises and propositions an explanation for evolutionary "pop-up" or spurting appearances. A saltationist inference has logically explained the construction of basic and elementary proto-forms of life; it has been argued that there are fundamental levels of predeveloped forms before we arrive at for example what can be referred to as an eye. We cannot have extreme hyperbolic and miraculous appearances of for example a modern day airplane, but there can be rudiment levels as pop-up entities.

It is argued that there must be gradual processual development before we can arrive at any or various complex objects. Gradualism becomes the key term since the concept of leap frogging can feasibly be remodeled and further deconstructed to smaller degrees and finite perception levels. Also, one could

Point A = Proto Form = Attributes TUVW
Point C = Intergraded Form = Attributes UVWX
Point E = Progressed Form = Attributes VWXY

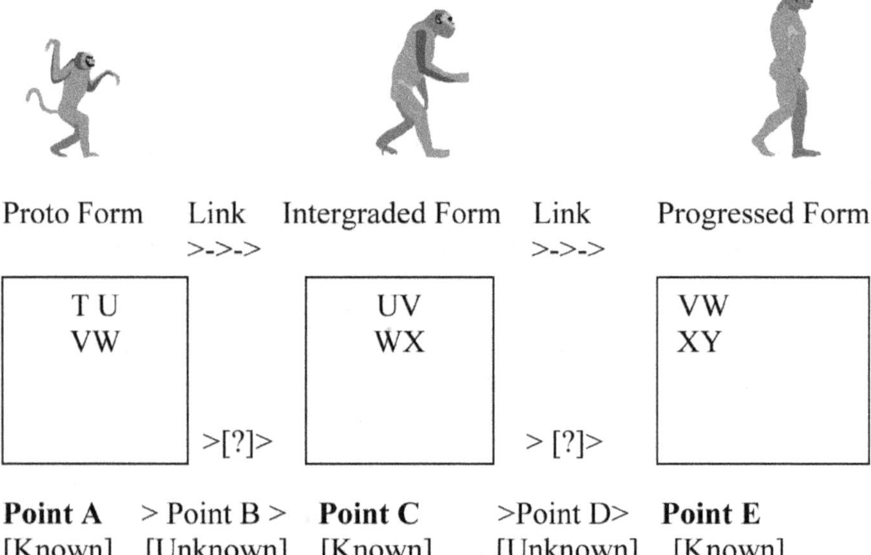

Figure 2.1. Structure of Analogical Inference. This depiction was created by the author.

include further along with the use of reason that our envisioning of a progressive sequential pattern teleologically accessed in the archaeological record makes sufficient the proof for perceived culminational autonomies to even a highly conscious and spiritual being.

Moreover, the disputing empiricist would comprehend the inclusion of a causal necessity as an unsightly metaphysical and innate annoyance. Empirically we find that what we do not still have is a point B (the link), and we should not make one up in our minds. We look and we find that all that we have in our ever (re)newed and (re)envisioned and (re)hypothesized and (re)analyzed past are all point A's and point C's. When we regard inference about the much long time-spanned teleology we must then consider that what we have are pocketed resultants of already changed forms. Or should they all, every single group, be construed as mixed hybridized monstrosities? All archaeological remains of teeth, bones, and skulls must be understood as once having existed within nature (within an environment) and no matter how cumbersome they may seem in comparison to later pre-human and proto-human models (for they all did exist for some time) they were harmoniously persisting throughout thousands and for some millions of years within their own respective time periods and to the empiricist singly and unconnected.

Let me turn to a famous eighteenth century Scottish philosopher named David Hume who would be described as an extreme empiricist and who presented a theory to combat rationalism run amok, let us turn to his theory here specifically entitled "constant conjunctions." According to Hume, when we constantly conjoin two objects we are really making a metaphysical inference. When Hume refers to metaphysical inference inference would mean that one object makes us expect the other, the sight of a point A form of development and the sight of a point C makes us envision or better yet await the sight of the intervening point B because we plainly see that there is a point C and we customarily come to look forward to the sought after point B.

Thus, A does not cause B but makes us await B which we now also inherently infer must have precursored point C for point A and point C cannot plainly be disjunctive punctualistic leaps for they have recognizable semblances or tendencies toward a progressive similitude. Semblances and similarities becomes a very important aspect in our philosophy because science has argued that nature has a great disdain for illogical entities that is why animals or rather living organisms most times die out because they in a sense do not maintain conformity. There is conformity in nature and there is a natural harmony that seems to exist. The concept of semblances and similarities works within that law of conformity and serves a purpose.

The extrapolated Hume-ian concept referred to as "constant conjunction" also reflects innateness about sequences and order. When we have disjunctive gaps we must see a logic, a B had come or we make out certain other types of ("imaginary") connectives between A and C and we go on to link A to C or require that there be a B and reconstruct an A > B > C connectivity and sometimes even a causality. What we make use of is rationalism in what assists in a "scientific explanation" for the persistence of tree shrews, prosimians, anthropoids, hominoids, hominines, and hominids. We have an A and C, E, G, I etc. therefore there must be a B, D, F, H and etc. and therefore A is connected to C and so on because we see physiological progress, and all our archaeological finds (teeth, bones, and skulls) ruminate in our mind and we must construct order via teleological inferences.

Science has searched for point Bs, Ds, Fs, Hs, etc. for over 100 years since Darwinian rationalism. Hume states, "[o]bjects have no discoverable connection together, nor is it from any other principle but custom operating upon the imagination, that we can draw any inference from the appearance of one to the experience of another."[5] Hume explains to us that what looks to us as a necessary connection among objects is really our ideas about the objects, that is to say that our perceptions are determined by our accustomed mind. As children we learn from the very beginning that we must place squares in square holes, we must place circles in circles, and so on and so on.

There must be order. We are rational as we look at the world and we must explain the world within a sense of rationality. Thus, irrationally descriptive human evolutionary explanation becomes unscientific. Subsequently, clinal species A and C must have had intergrades as they morphologically moved through a logical connective series of demes. The key issue then becomes where are the fossils that personify hybrids? Or can we identify the suture zones that connect segregates A, C, E, G, I, etc. etc. etc.?[6] Or what if we are all hybrids, intergrades, and mixtures and have been from the start?

ANTHROPOMORPHIC WHYS

Prehuman to human intermediates will probably never be clearly seen for what we seek now more than prehuman to human intermediates is to understand the overall intent behind the resultant designed form that is called human. For what will end all research is not the answer to "how," but completing the answer to "why" which has always maintained a potentiality of halting science. Why is humanity endowed with such an impeccable functional design that is not only anatomically efficient, but also spiritual and that continues to always amaze? Science once considered by Hume as a nonreligion, can be considered by a more secular observant populus as functionalistically explanatory and in a sense its use can be construed as modernity's religion. Our present day dependency to understand world phenomena has transformed science into scientific religiosity.

Modern-day science demystifies many prior unexplained natural phenomena and perhaps also it may one day come to totally explain the ultimate answer to the meaning of life. When we search for answers purposiveness always seems to reside in the silent background, it always hides in an *obscurum* in *silentio* fashion. When we do search for humanity's significance (whether perceived as angelic or destructive) we cannot rightfully ascertain humanity's intent other than seeing ourselves as somewhat tangential to the divine. Thus, as time continues science must always fall back to yet another "(re)" envisioned rationalism.

Secular science wants to validate itself and wants to give credence to all that it perceives and explains. According to a perceptive biologist what science needs are better-equipped anthropologists, it seems that even a better "molecular anthropology" should be created so that science can work through discoveries with a generalististic purpose in mind and with a "critical analytical and ethnographic eye."[7] It seems that as the mechanics of science becomes more advanced what we need is yet another specialized anthropology to deal with the participation of science because a science based molecular genetics has a sway that can "make a familiar fact seem unfamiliar" and what also becomes more troubling is that molecular genetics can "give biases and opinions the sing of scientific authority."[8] What we really need is a meta-anthropological inquiry, an anthropology of anthropology; this of course would mean more than just a philosophy of science, but a social policy on science for what troubles us most is not the falsehood tendencies of scientific facts, but the suavity of scientific authority.

NOTES

1. See Diamond's prologue on p. 2 and although we are all three almost identical, the most intelligent one of the three, the third chimpanzee, has (1) opted to dissect, (2) chosen to cut off the hands, (3) injected with the AIDS virus, and (4) ruined the habitats of the other two related kin, p. 214.
2. Wenke, p. 80 on Schwalbe and human stages.
3. See Abend's (1929) article in *The New York Times* for Peking Man allusions, see Hall's (1929) article in *The New York Times* for presumptions about a Pacific Coast human fossil find, see Strickland (1979) who argues (p. 54) that "our ancestors" began in a dry Mediterranean area and then ran up to the hills, and see Maynard (2001) in *The Times* (London) for DNA scientific notions about Australian human origins.
4. Several British intellectuals had attested to the supposed link, and here I'll just name two key suspects from an implicated group, there was a lawyer and ambitious amateur researcher named Charles Dawson and a far too entrenched to recant scholar and at the time geological director by the name of Arthur Smith Woodward. These two learned men had given critical support, please see book by Walsh. There will be more said of the group, but for now I will state that obviously the sensationalized specimen was exposed as a fraud. Unfortunately, a mystery still remains as to who specifically was the culprit/s that masterminded the entire Piltdown forgery.
5. Russell, p. 665.

6. Simons (1972), p. 33–34. Simons cautions about the problems of trying to work out time-successions of ancestor-descendant links from extant to extinct forms.
7. Marks, p. 67.
8. *Ibid.*

Chapter Three

Black Diffusion

THE BLACK ENTITY

Certain specific fictional literary texts will help to explain an aspect regarding color. In an all-perfect world black is just a color and nothing else—neither more nor less. But unfortunately to a Western European-based intelligentsia the black represents something more. Black existence represents a backdrop *sapiens*, i.e. a standard by which we can measure comparative and designed forms of modern humanity. Allow me here to avert to nineteenth century (1853) Western intellectualism, allow me to turn to Gobineau as a prime example of biased color spectrum analysis where when speaking of yellowness he is compelled to refer to blackness as he takes an unencumbered stance to defend whiteness:

> The yellow race presents itself like the antithesis of this type [black race]. The skull, in lieu of the black race being pointed in the back part, points precisely in the front part. The forehead, wide, bony, often projecting, is developed in height, and its weight is set upon a triangular face; the nose and the chin do not show none of the course and the rough projection which notates the black race. There is a general tendency to obesity which is not a whole trait in this particular case, nevertheless it is encountered much frequently with the yellow tribes which are rarities in the others. *The yellow* race has not much of bodily strength and has a deposition for apathy. In morality, the yellow race has none of those strange excesses that are common with the black race. [1]

The "black" is the standard "*negre*" and the "yellow" is a measured "*jaune*" and both exist under the supposedly superior and useful European anthropometric model, the "yellow" is not entirely quite as animalistic as the "black," "*generale a…obesite…*," but at times the "yellow" is similar in degenerativeness as the "black," "*si communs chez les Melaniens,*" and ultimately, the "yellow" is enclosed within a nullifying melanism. Gobineau's "yellow" has a black inclusiveness of color; the "yellow" is inevitably scaled down to the typically white perceived abysmal blackness. Once again working within Eurocentric construction on otherness all that can be negated must always come down to terminus blackness. Consequentially, what we have is a black/white polar extreme in which to, not only popularly but also scholarly, gauge the world. It is the black/white dichotomy that concerns Westernism, and it is a polar extreme color spectrum that is implemented in historic human social associations. White Western humanity, so it seems, has been plagued by the consciousness of color for a very long time. Gobineau continues with his defense of whiteness as he constructs a literary black-white comparative belief:

> The white race is further distinguished by the singular love for life. They know that better, how to make use of it. As it seems they attribute a higher price to it, they spare more of it, in they themselves and in others. They are cruel, when they practice cruelty, they are conscious of their practice, it is very doubtful that such consciousness exists in the black race. At the same time, these things occupy life, which is precious to them; they are discovering the reasons of living without complaining. The first of these motives is honor, which under various names, has occupied an enormous place in the ideas of the species from the beginning. I should need not add that the word honor and the notion of civilizing which are self-contained, equally, is unknown both to the yellow and the black races.[2]

In attempting to distinguish and make certain an innateness of whiteness Westernism is constantly absorbed by how black culture works and by a preoccupation with visions about dysfunctional blackness, and except for those few like Gobineau who are bold enough to present belief constructs that have remained in the white mind, most would rather maintain discreteness and refrain from such blatant perspectives. Moreover, most have remained and have passed along the practice of what I call modern-day indiscrete negation of a nonwhite otherness.

When we review white intellectualism that particularly speaks of origins of cultural ideas and independent developments we again find that there is always a subliminal force at work that reproduces perceptions of blackness. There are unyielding forces against perceptions of black independency. When I refer to black independency I speak about black cultural origination and its black cultural diffusive affects that undoubtedly spread to white cultures and that ultimately become unacknowledged as black derived.

Back in the 1950s in the old cultural anthropological studies that tackled issues of black-against-white political struggles, we can assert that there were deep-rooted differences in various levels of comprehension and that this warring duality existed not only in the civil rights arena, but also at the anthropological/sociological intellectual levels. That is to say that all literature in the sciences and social sciences can be construed and interpreted as being politicizing. In 1951 a great white-male thinker and Western anthropologist by the name of Leslie White from the University of Michigan reviewed in a generalized sense the various theoretical aspects expounded in the early twentieth century on the derivation of overall cultural changes. In talking about the Boasian relativistic school of thought, he goes on to state,

> What the Boasians did here was to confuse the culture history of a people with the evolution of culture as such. They argued, for example, that because some African Negro tribes obtained iron-working by diffusion it was not necessary for "all peoples to go through the same stages of cultural development," and that therefore the theories of the evolutionists were fallacious. But the evolutionists never claimed that "every people had to go through the same stages of cultural development"; they merely argued that metallurgy or clan organization or writing was something that had to be evolved, or developed, from earlier stages or forms. To the evolutionist it made no difference whether a given people that they were concerned obtained a trait by diffusion or developed it indigenously; it was the evolution of the culture that they were concerned with, not the cultural experiences of this or that tribe.[3]

Disregarding for the moment the direct defense of unbiased evolutionism, this passage is a clear representation of how symbolically negated blackness, the "African Negro," had become. Again, from a Western (European) perception blackness is discretely perceived in a hierarchical construct at the bottom of worldly cultural existence. The "African Negro" becomes the standard by which modern Western intellectualism works at assessing civilizational progress or evolutionistic activity and theoretically demarcates the line between human significance and inhuman primitivism. Once again the "African Negro" is indirectly gauged as a form to measure a process. In attacking Boasian relativism, White works at making his point and excluding the crux of the universal problem. Western intellectualism works discretely and wants the world to perceive propped up fairness and unbiasness. We are continually instructed to not be concerned about "African Negro" and such experiential matters and concentrate on the "man," that is to say concentrate on a skewed humanity that forever defines blackness.

Finally, in White's article, he goes on to conclude, "[a]nd we may be sure that whatever fads and fashions may come and go in anthropology, the problems of evolution and diffusion will remain with us for a long time to come."[4] Here in an article on cultural derivation White reverts to the age-old contention that involves the traditionalized blackless evolution and disregarded black diffusion. Overall, White wants us to note that cultural change occurs and evolutionism and diffusionism never should be conflictual elements, one produces and the other spreads in what can be interpreted as a supposedly non-offensive colorless pattern. What White failed to note was that to the black consciousness it is not discrete and it cannot remain disregarded. Western knowledge becomes excruciating to understand. White, the Western intellectual patriarch of cultural anthropology, continues and avoids the real contentions against such thoughts about Elliot Smith's Pan-Egyptian theory or what he footnotes as "Asiatic influences" and comparisons between Southern Asian and Middle American similarities.[5] White had keenly circumvented real engaged discussion within the realm of what I will refer to as the persistency of black-white polarity.

White's Westernism must reason through perceptions of blackness that obstinately remain consistent in a white creative expansiveness. Primarily, Western scholarship will always eloquently work black entities and creativeness into an occlusive background. Westernism can only reason through portrayals of blackness that sub-functions within a white aggrandizement. Any pro-black counter-arguments and black-independent, counter-white belief structures as self-derived and self-existent are merely presented as implausible and unsound or at best parenthetical knowledge. Although blackness almost interminably becomes mystified and speculative, a staunch black re-infusionism always becomes penetrable and thus resurfaces amid a disgruntled European derived tradition.

European American realization of black existentialism that is directed at an audience is a never-ending endeavor. In October 28, 1959, an American citizen by the name of John Howard Griffin began a voyage into blackness. Subsequently, he went on and published a book about his personal experiences titled *Black Like Me*. He wanted to find out what living in the nonwhite American South would feel like. He was astounded and dismayed by what he experienced. Griffin begins the preface of his book with, "This may not be all of it. It may not cover all the questions, but it is what it is like to be a Negro in a land where we keep the Negro down."[6] Griffin or rather as he refers to himself, "Negro Griffin," went and looked out from within blackness at the injustices of whiteness, and he wanted to actualize a grievous existence.[7] Griffin envisions that his work would bring black betterment and respectability and he also clings to the hopes and dreams of a black and white coexistent utopia. He proscribes this instruction specifically to an African American audience:

> The Negro's only salvation from complete despair lies in his belief, the old belief of his forefathers, that these things are not directed against him personally, but against his race, his pigmentation. His mother or aunt or teacher long ago carefully prepared him explaining that he as an individual can live in dignity, even though he as a Negro cannot. "They don't do it to you because you're Johnny—they don't know you. They do it against your Negro-ness."[8]

Griffin's mentioned sojourn like (the freedom fighting) John Brown's long past liberalism worked at presenting black idealization that forever persists within a historic, revisited and profound white conscious perspective of downtrodden blackness. In Griffin's addendum to the second edition of the same book we discover that Griffin himself transforms and understands that the Negro's physical liberation has brought on varying observances and concerns, the Negro now has changed and Griffin regards them as no longer being Negro, but black.[9] It is a blackness that has finally been revealed and liberated. The Negro just like the publicly vociferous times of the civil rights activist and populist struggles has disappeared into a time past.

Nevertheless, Griffin's literary text was as revealing as *Uncle Tom's Cabin* where Harriet Beecher Stowe in a prior age and time and in a span of a little over one hundred years (1853 to 1959) had helped to bring black realization. Stowe helped to popularize feelings against slavery to a white audience via a literary art form. A sense of black injurious existence was expressed in literary form, but long ago it was a female writer of European descent who spread the word on a discerned blackness. While white males entertained in black face laughing and pretending in creative minstrel form to induce yet another different kind of *presbyopia* of blackness, a white audience yearned for yet other instances of black penetration. There will always be a need to depict, in literary and entertaining *Gestalt*, the contemporaneous harrowing sentiment of blackness. Being black takes its toll in a disempowering Westernizing world with its great white Western *imperium* that remains gluttonous while it rules and that becomes better skilled at improvising discreetness and that also mandates better scientific and self-validated based assumptions to what appropriately can be otherwise called global and perpetual European derived control.

Please note here that this enquiry does not present a staunch resolute perception about blackness and does not endeavor to reinstitute late nineteenth century Ethiopianism and or early twentieth century pan-Africanism which had once found their peaks in the 1890s and early1900s.[10] Moreover, this enquiry does not discredit Christianized Ethiopianism or political pan-Africanism, this enquiry contends multiplicity over divisive idealizations (black and/or white) which have not helped overall the human fragmental existence. Conclusively, the enquiry identifies geometric retrospective intellectualism and notes the past historic Ethiopianists, pan-Africanists, black monumentalists, and/or black exceptionalists have attempted to create separate spaces that were not decisively intent on erasing harmful creative constructs.[11] Ideals for a freedom-loving space have been discredited by intra-warring and self-combative African Liberias historically in various instances. Liberia is a free country where a notion of autonomy was once formerly used as a ruse to entice innocent people in order to better the white American condition and in order to transplant miniaturized versions of Americanism.

Western manufactured African civilizations have continuously suffered from greedy capitalistic existentialism that plague the indigenous and purposefully repress innate African mannerisms of unity.

There are various other notions of blackness. To create black can have other meanings other than what has been denoted by science, by anthropology and generally by the "intellectual thinking" (or rather Western thinking) people in their clean white coats. There is the nihilistic blackness which has been customarily historicized and traditionally perceived as credible. Even a demystifying Frank M. Snowden, a "Harvard-educated" scholar who worked within the nurturing halls of a black university had presented the philological and invariably creative ideal that the past had existed without color and without prejudice. A colorless and pristine antiquity is what Western intellectualism interminably strives to present in order to set the stage for a harmoniously social multicultural future co-existence. An ancient and idyllic world is commonly presented where Hellenism and Romanism were fair as fair can be and as fair as our democratic and pure "apple pie" Americanism. Primarily, Snowden presents a Western fundamentally and intellectually regurgitated and fanciful concept where an ancient world exists without prejudice and without color, a utopic antiquity without the evil modern sense of racism.[12]

According to Snowden who helps to build upon a European derived construction, European discrimination had not originated during the Greco-Roman times. Plato, Aristotle, Plutarch, etc. had never denied blackness. The ancients, who are presented in the same traditionalized form of nineteenth-century thought where the Greeks in particular are perceived as the naïve and unaware little children of the great fatherly Western civilization, had not derived a pejorative blackness. Perhaps it would seem best to bring invisibility to blackness in antiquity too. Perhaps the present world would be better off to construe a Western ancient past inconsequential of color biases. Thus, let us erase blackened Egypt, blackened Crete, blackened Athena, blackened Augustine, blackened antiquity, and black connectivity and instead let us just keep black holes, black mail, black Sunday, black eye, black sin, etc. etc. etc.

Once again considering the Western bipolar condition and color perceptions this enquiry turns to what can be interpreted as an ever-changing historical process of transforming the goodness of blackness into whiteness. Whiteness will always transpire to goodness. And as time passes what do we make of the black? According to Oliver the present world must contend with the evil of historiographical "metapmorph" treatments.[13] Oliver presents the idea that all black beings, i.e., any black form that does exist within the synchronous realm of goodness as time moves forward, will always be transformed into whiteness. As time passes forward certain intellectual thinkers of the past will work at changing beings. As with Cadmus, Achilles, Jesus, etc. etc. etc., so too even by another two hundred years or more the Reverend

Doctor Martin Luther King may also be perceived as being white or at linked in some form or way to whiteness.[14]

The dominant whiteness influential and perceptional process has always decided what will be negated and thus blackened. The black in white perception is traditionally viewed as an incessant negativity. Black American conscious movements, propounded extensively by an African American post-reconstructionist, W.E.B. Du Bois, and the like, brought on knowledge of not only black psychological impediments, but also revelation of intra-black polarity. Struggle within the black self is propelled by a forever differentiating Westernism that has extended to an unfortunate digressive cognition and it seems more a psychiatric condition than anything else. The divided oneness of the black soul cannot possibly move forward without having to abide by the forces of both selves that are forever working at pulling the one black soul apart.

There is also the black struggle against self-misrecognition and worldly invisibility that has been a long drawn out competitive endeavor. To better elaborate this point this enquiry turns to Ralph Ellison's *Invisible Man*. In Ellison's book we come to a prophetic scene where the protagonist drives up to the Long Island plant and sees a high electric sign that states, "Keep America Pure with Liberty Paint." In this profit-making and successful paint factory the black protagonist obtains a job and learns how to make paint. The best white paint in the world is made here, and as the story continues we learn that each bucket of that infamous "Optic White" paint requires ten drops of black paint.

We learn that it takes blackness to create whiteness; we learn that it takes black to create pure and good white, "white as George Washington."[15] In Ellison we learn that the black, factory-basement worker named Lucius Brockway unconsciously slaves away and helps to produce the best white selling paint in the world.[16] Brockway also entertains in minstrel form as he tells the protagonist that he helped to make the company slogan "If It's Optic White, It's the Right White."[17] The key point I am making with Ellison's novel is that it takes black to produce white, an essential hybridity, and an ecumenical internality. Similarly, the necessity of black/white co-existent and human intrinsic entity can also be found as a prehistoric axiomatic universalism that has been denied and unfortunately refuted by those who have created biased and historicized one-dimensional anthropological perceptions.

Black diffusion, the process where blackness has passed along throughout all of humanity's existence on this planet, through a black geographic African centrality that had remained pinpointed even while in the earliest geologic form from Pangea to its subsequent break into Laurasia and what I call black Gondwanaland and so forth. Black spreads from an African base is what this work contends. For since the very beginning of time natural selection of entities has sought to replicate and survive on earth in multiple derivational forms and persists within one planet. It is the nature of evolution to persevere in whatever transitory entity that it can. If the first is black then their derivatives are considered black based. As we consider the propensity of every living creature to survive and to replicate with some change here and there then we must see that it is black diffusion with its embedded black spirit that must lie within every human soul.

UTILITARIAN UNIVERSALISM

When we review morphological transformations as regards general progression from a small creature to what will be referred to here as prehumanity, we must delve into the rationalization of its purpose. Some evolutionists see the world as existing within an economic modeled social setting; they use the concept of "utility function" to help describe the purpose of life. The "utility function" is a term specifically borrowed from economics by Richard Dawkins, the eminent "Oxford trained" gradualist defender, in an innovative attempt to explain the complexities of natural selection and evolution. The term refers to a utilitarian striving in order to maximize something, as for example trying to obtain the "greatest happiness for the greatest number."[18]

According to Dawkins the purposeful function for all God's smallest and greatest creatures is the single "Utility Function" of life that is to simply state that the "Utility Function" of life is critical for DNA survival. He asserts that "the DNA that remains locked up in living bodies" such as in cheetahs, gazelles, antelopes, tigers etc. etc. all are fighting fiendishly to keep alive. Genes trapped in these living bodies (and somewhat immediately seeming indifferent to the outside violent world) are always maximizing their selfish welfare at their own level. They are "programming unselfish cooperation, or even self-sacrifice, by the organism at its level. But group welfare is always a fortuitous consequence, not a primary drive." There is individualized greed behind it all, the greed to persevere and the drive to pass on one's own genetic structure. This motivational force explains the meaning behind Dawkins' term "the selfish gene."[19]

This life-endeavoring programming is inherent in the natural selection process. Natural selection is DNA interminably working out multiple fashions for replication and perpetuation. Combined and recombined molecular structures of GATC are what we find in life that is to say that "[a]ll the organs and limbs of animals, the roots, leaves and flowers of plants; all eyes and brains and minds, and even fears and hopes, are the tools by which successful DNA sequences lever themselves into the future."[20]

PERCEPTIONS ON ORIGINS

And so, the search for intermediaries will not be quite distinctively found because what is defined is what can be considered soulful and plasmic diffusion of genetic types. What Dawkins does not include in the human spectrum is that what we have are black spreads without disjunctive originating points and what is found are not separate autonomies and pop-up independencies, but expansive billowing black spiritual fluidity. As we come to understand human interconnectedness we perceive that there is no ancestral mitochondrial Eve or a singly whole-developed Adam and Eve, but multiple, forward-flowing intermediates that encompass hybridity at undetectable levels and this recombinant striving primarily stems from a black origination.

Thus, black rooted transformational becomes so gradual that we will never come to see the ideal specimen such as a half-ape/half-human combined entity. We will never find the originating point or idea, such origins are always preceded and withheld by multiple concurrence. What is being stated here is that originating points of entities such as defining the locality of creation will always remain suspect because of the universalism of a rooted blackness that maintains a constant propensity to survive and to replicate and so we are left with inherent forever striving encaptulatedness. And a white intellectualizing prevalence forever disavows the black. Simultaneity can and must always be considered in a black gradual transformance of not only organisms as with hominids, but also the all-embracing black origins of humanity. Conjectures about prehuman or human origin localities will always accrue as science expands and works at more improvised creativities.

Traditionally, as initially presented by an authoritative German named Franz Weidenreich, in the 1940s, most scholars had adhered to the biblically inspired orthogenesis model, which held that there were four parallel lines of separate origins for *Homo sapiens*. They explicitly recognized and held separate the Australian, the Mongolian, the African, and the Eurasian lines. These prehistoric (internally and autonomously changing) ancestral lines of descent were believed to have traveled as far back as the *Pithecanthropicus* point, which means the point where the encapsulated ape-human and transforming entity purportedly breaks apart.[21] It was the German anatomist, a student of the very same Schwalbe (mentioned previously here in Chapter 3), Franz Weidenrich who did archaeological work in China and who devised a polycentric evolutionistic model that precursored the present human multiregional continuity theory, a concept about human race or subspecies evolution that can be considered as the interdisciplinary union between modern populational biology and traditional polycentric theory.[22] Such revised, (re)envisioned, discretely creative scientific interdisciplinary studies have always, and will probably still reproduce more harm than good.

Anthropological ideas about origins with their differing titles and pontificating paradigms have led to archaeological crusades to seek origins in Europe, Asia, Australia, and even America. It seems that all polycentric theorists with their strongly idealized and divided origins have only complicated human social matters. One could also add that multiregionalistic theories have only helped to further instill much of the fragmental and separatistic *Zeitgeist* that permeates throughout a world still very nationalistically and geographically boundary obsessed. It seems that difficulties in finding origins and perceptions of origins and scientific designs on the past have solely produced more inventive explanations that have not helped to produce better human cohesiveness, a dire scientific problem indeed.

NOTES

1. Gobineau (1853) Vol. I p. 352, La race jaune se presente comme l'antithese de ce type. Le crane, au lieu d'etre rejete en arriere, se porte precisement en avant. Le front, large, osseux, souvent saillant, developpe en hauteur, plombe sur un facies triangulaire, ou le nex et le menton ne montrent aucune des saillies grossieres et rudes qui font remarquier le negre. Une tendance generale a l' obesite n'est pas la un trait tout a fait special, purtant il se recontre plus frequemment chez les tribus jaunes que dans les autres varieties. Peu de vigueur physique des dispositions a l'apathie. Au moral, aucun de ces exces estranges, si communs chez les Melaniens.
2. *Ibid.*, p. 354, Les blancs se distinguent encore par un amour singulier de la vie. Il parait que, sachant mieux en user, ils lui attribuent plus de-prix, ils la menagent advantage, en eux-memes et dans les autres. Leur cruaute, quand elle s'exerce, a la conscience de ses exces, sentiment tres-problematique ches les noirs. En meme temps, cette vie occupee, qui leur est si precieuse, ils ont decouvert des raisons de la livrer sans murmure. Le premier de ces mobiles, c'est l'honneur, qui, sous des noms a peu pres pareils, a occupe une enorme place dans les idees, depuis le commencement de l'espece. Je n'ai pas desoin d'ajouter que ce mot d'honneur et la notion civilizatrice qu'il renferme sont, egalement, inconnus aux jaunes et aux noirs.
3. White, p. 218.
4. *Ibid.*
5. *Ibid.*
6. Griffin, preface.
7. *Ibid.*, p. 133.
8. *Ibid.*, p. 48.
9. *Ibid.*, p. 208.
10. See Gruesser p. 23.
11. *Ibid.*, *passim* and in particular p. 157 for use of the terms Ethiopianist, monumentalism, and exceptionalism. Please note that these terms are not being centrally used in this enquiry for critical purposes.
12. Snowden, both books.
13. Oliver, p. 50 and p. 54.
14. *Ibid.*, p. 34.
15. Ellison p. 201.
16. *Ibid.*, p. 217.
17. *Ibid.*, p. 218.
18. Dawkins (1995), p. 103–104.
19. *Ibid.*, p. 122.
20. *Ibid.*, p. 150.
21. Tattersall (1988), p. 213.
22. Wolpoff (1997), p. 31.

Chapter Four

Envisioning Prebeginnings

HUMANITY'S PREBEGINNINGS

Hundreds of millions of years after a protocell appears on earth life is re-created in a preponderance of diversities. It all begins with preliminary atmospheres that mixed and precipitated into an ecologically and a perfectly structured earth. Primitive atmospheres helped to transform various sized molecules that then helped to create protocells that led to prokayotes and that then transformed their way into eukayotes and that subsequently arrived at multicellular organisms. It is amazing to note that all these perceived transformative processes perpetuate on and on and on as life continues to gain forward. Life moved forward right up to our present time when we arrive at modern humanity with all its other coexisting and mutually persistent creatures that competitively struggle to maintain within an ever-increasing and ever-destructive human populational world. Permutated trends in life have taken place and it seems that since the beginning of contemplative human's existence there has been an established requisite to understand all these world-life changes, i.e. we strive to know in order to accurately understand our place within this cherished world we call earth and to accept our seemingly blessed and complex perpetuity.

Humanity has necessitated an explanatory answer for its own substantiality. Our life's appearance now in post-postmodernity has been viewed from a Western scientific community and from a now interminable and also protean and reconstructive science, as being culminational and purposeful, that is to state a lucid scientific process reproduces an expositional system that commonly self-identifies and (re)creates "a white analyzing" human origins construct. It is a persistent Western science that dominantly stabilizes a tenaciously paradigmatic and self-derived white transformative phenomenon. We now have arrived at scientific explanations that stand supremely and imperatively cybernetic and that always remain self-refuting, non-ceasing and for useful reasons nonblack.

In general, what is humanity? How was it that we came to be? A post-nineteenth century and (re)newed anthropological science has defined the human as intelligent, self-aware, social, tool using and political, and along with these positive characterizations about humanity paleoanthropological knowledge has gone further and has pointed out the primordial benefits that were inherited by humanity from the beast. Paleo and neoprimatologists alike uphold experimental and validated scientific theories concerning human extrapolations of various particular social (or behavioral) and physical (or anatomical) capacities that have been proposed as being (again in a theoretical sense) passed on from beasts.

These scientific interpreters of human evolutionism, in expressly paleoprimatological, and or in general primatological terms, serve as narrators about humanity's origin and they have come to present an elaborate and creative portrayal of humanity's linkage through the usage of a reified, descriptive and reformative past, i.e. a prehuman past that has been ascertained from the fossil record and from extant forms of apes. From the fossil record our keen and insightful paleoprimatologists go on to describe the initial anatomical and characteristic borrowings and substitutions which led to humanity and also they have identified humanity's fundamental progress from very small scurrying and fortunate mammalian creatures that date way back to sometime slightly before 65 million years ago.

EVOLUTIONARY DEPICTIONS

Natural selection's universal mechanism is all to blame since its discovery, i.e. since an eighteenth century's enlightened and unyielding European man's contemplative and radiating moment *in memoriam.*[1] Since the eighteenth century, it seems that (in a conglomerated sense) European knowledge has repeatedly expounded evolutionist doctrines and has propelled a credulous modernity to accept the scientific construct that human transformations, as with most other life forms in general, have become random and yet purposeful. It seems that attested from the review of combined geologic rocks and fossilized bones and through a self-regulating assessment of notated prehistoric ages, retrospective science has maintained that humanity has continued over a 65 million year descent away from nature.

An evolutionary history depicted from the fossil record discloses evidentiary progress. Also, it now becomes obvious that various sciences (molecular biological included) have confirmed an ape-human ancestral commonality that throughout a pre-eighteenth century and historic past had tentatively remained hidden that is until the validating commencement of persuasive, edifying, and taphonomical-sustained rocks. What once would have been considered to be nontime-bound rocks to a previous scientific observer (pre-eighteenth century), would now come to be transformed into conceptualized meaning and would come to be principally deciphered by a nineteenth century and newly established and geologically assisted *archaeologia.*

In regards to the preliminary beginnings of the origins of humanity, paleoprimatological Western science has found appearances and disappearances of archaic primate life connected to sedimentary beds and geologic rocks, and all of it in retrospect to prehumanity's theoretical upbringing. Some would contend that the appearances and disappearances of prehistoric primates have helped to propose humanity's logical transformation from scurrying little creatures that are seen as being connected from the precursory pre-primates right up on through to the transitionally encumbered prehumans (hominids) and then onto the properly upright walking humans. Western science has always esteemed and reconditioned that humanity is advancement forward in the struggle for supreme existence.

Some would reason that we walk on our hind legs with our vertebral columns held upright because of a specific past teleology, i.e., reconsidered, evolutionary persistency or utilitarian functionalism, and some would further contend that we must have been given large brains in relation to our body sizes (referred to as the encephalization quotient) for a sensible logic for why else would humanity require such cranial spatial capacities grown to over 1400 cubic centimeters. One could further rationalize that all that dendritic and synaptic cranial spatial increase for simply overall enlarged bestial animality would seem quite wasteful and foolish. Western science explains that natural selection is never needless and wasteful. The same kind of syllogism on anatomical advancement can be used when we query Western science about life-form's simple-to-complex evolutionary, morphological and physical characterizations. All kinds of anatomical changes accrue even before we became humanly distinct from lesser forms of beasts as hominids, and we must remember that no matter how bodily inadequate hominids may seem today, nonetheless they existed for a long period of time. Variant hominid forms are noted to have persisted within a homeostatic and an advantageous ecological niche for over two million years. Therefore, this prehuman-to-human transmorphic process requires thoughtful consideration.

PRIMATES AS ANIMALIA PRIMA

In this continuous *explans* that scrutinizes within a generalized paleoprimatological base, this next juncture advances to intended extinct *Primate* forms to express a comparative perception on overall prehuman-to-human evolutionary developments. The enquiry turns to certain archaic *Primate* forms, addresses typological inferences on fossil remains, and elaborates on the scientific theoretical affirmations made concerning humanity's origin.

Descriptive scientific narratives concerning the origins of *Primate* life forms have gone on for an extremely long time since the 1730s and since the "Uppsala-trained" Swedish naturalist named Carl von Linné or Carolus Linnaeus, the father of taxonomy and a life-long lover of botany, who first helped to categorize the natural world back in 1735 with his *Systema Naturae*. Again, here is another instance where questions and speculations about human origins and beast-to-human boundaries fall within the sphere of the "creationist-evolutionist" debacle. Back then we not only have explanations about human links to the *amoebae* and early aquatic life forms that were intensely contested but also here we have creationism combating Western science's use of the proto-typic and precursory little mammalian rodent-like creatures as a prominent and anthropomorphically compact analogue. The *Bible* does not mention primatological transformational developments, but the book of *Genesis* in the beginning particularly *Book 1:25* does mention that God created animals, birds, livestock and creatures before humanity. In a general way there seems to be a progressive order to the sequences of all living creatures.

Scientifically, the little mammalian survivors have been presented as the earliest if not the originated *Primates* that helped to continue the evolutionary process that arrives at humanity. Science has pointed to these creatures and disgruntled creationists have countered-argued that in general scientific explanations have answered the mechanics in a self-assuming and self-debunking manner, but what science has always failed to do is to answer the simplified and the somewhat childlike and inquisitive "why" question. According to creationists, scientific explications have solely gone on to demystify the complex process of morphology without any primatological standalone specimen that is inherently a proper explicative of convincible transmorphic rationalism.

When we review the extinct prehuman protodevelopmental progression within the Order of *Primates* according to creationism, certain questions will always continue to accrue. Despite all the scientific technological advancement that has helped to better understand nature, the unanswerable "why" question still maintains constancy. For example, in regards to paleoprimatology, why then did the *Tupaiia* begin to have a smaller olfactory apparatus than the other primitive insectivores back in the Cretaceous Period? Or better yet, why did *Tupaiia* have rudimentary primate-like dentition, i.e. before the arrival of, or at the brink of, subsequent full-fledged primates? Or rather, in an elaborated sense, why did prehumans (hominids)? Why did the relativistic prehumans who have been linked through a *prospective* expansive stasis come to have analogical physical characterizations to both early *Primate* forms and humans?

Moreover, why did extinct processual prehumans who came after the variegated pre- and proto-primate forms, or for that matter extensively, anthropoids (hominids, again in particular), come to have increased cortex regions (ever intent on surpassing a cerebral Rubicon of 500 cubic centimeters), and further reduced canines, and further enlarged pharynxes (the section of the throat located between the vocal cords and the oral cavity) than their less weighty and more obsolete relative primates? Science has explained the process of how it is that life-form appearances ecologically induced come to change, but the creationist would still contend that what scientific narrators are reciting is a conglomerated story about how a modern and secularized natural selective divinity rationally orchestrates and designs behind every created being. The Intelligent design of *Primates* for the most cerebrally potent and efficient living beings still remains investigative.

It should be noted here that the term *Primates* derived from the Latin root word primus meaning "first" and it was the name borrowed from Medieval Latin by Carolus Linnaeus back in 1758. The term means "chieftains" or the "first ones" as it is defined in the *Cambridge Encyclopedia.*[2] The word primate also can be construed in an ecclesiastical sense just as in the primate or the archbishop who is ranked first among the local bishops. Primates or chieftains were precisely what the taxonomic order was titled because humanity had been daringly categorized within it. It had become the "first order" because humans, who also fall under the *Primates* Order, are considered just that, the leaders of all other life forms. We determine here that just as in the commencement of the Roman Empire Octavian, the first Augustus, proclaimed himself *civis princeps*, "the first citizen," so too did European Linnaeus come to categorize a specific humanity as the first (and foremost) life form of all life forms in an hierarchical order that also placed the black at the footing of the human category.[3]

In a supreme sense Linnaeus, as instructed in *Genesis 2:19–20*, had become the initial sagacious man who named the world for long-awaited modernity, he had become (metaphorically) the world endowed Adam who principally stated, "Let it be proclaimed" that monkey, ape and "man" will stand as primary natural beings. From such a testament on existences it can be gathered that to name the sky, or for that matter to categorize almost every living thing in nature, is to take part in the creation of all living and dead entities in erstwhile unspecified worlds. A recognizable world is created simply because the entire world from a designated point of view will come to be understood within a Linnaean perspective, the very same Linnaean ideal that has bestowed Western labels and titles on a natural world formerly perceived as wild, disordered, disconnected, and black.

This enquiry reiterates that this exegesis with all its critiques on Westernism is primarily an analyzation of traditionalized intellectual constructions of blackness. We will keenly understand paleoprimatology or paleontological narrations established from a scientific primer and from an embedded and fluidic "European-male" aesthetic base. The key element in comprehending our general paleoprimatological analysis is that humanity's progressivity is now incorporated into a science that has come to better systematize and to better synthesize a humanly guided and controlled nature. It seems that because of an antiquated 1758 Linnaean labelization modernity has compounded and has further developed an eased eye on a palatable natural world, a world in which "man's" nonconnectivity to the beast has now transformed to a noncombative and interrelated but yet supremacist hierarchical construct. The little scurrying creatures (tree shrews) of the wild now take center stage and take their representational role in a well-ordered and devisable nature.

Scientific questions continue to come up and paleoprimatology has gone on to answer descriptively and elaborately many transformances about prehumanity. But yet again, the creationists continue to quail, "What of the interminable why?" One would want to know why did *Tupaiaformes* (tree shrews) begin with a middle ear design different from those of other insectivores and begin to show resemblances to primates. Why did primates leap from preprimate-like forms in what has been considered a chanced-based prehistoric flash? Why did prehumanity leap right from archaic primates within a geologic time span that could also be considered an instantaneous prehistoric moment?

Lastly, what remains unanswered is why then was prehumanity brewed with some of the ingredients borrowed from the ecologically well-established small mammalian creatures, that is to say small creatures that grew and grew and grew throughout a slow moving stasis? Why then these specific creatures who would come to have superb environmental feasibility and who would achieve the best imaginative maneuverability, once initially on the ground, and then up on to trees to return back to the ground and only logically and morphologically in a larger and weightier form?

CONTENDING BRAINS

The "whys" abound. They become endless. Again, why did primates begin with tree shrews? Or rather anachronistically, why did humanity's predevelopment begin with early primates? Alternatively, why did natural selection, whatever that multiple and scientifically described omnipotence may be, and however painstakingly slow it may seem, rationally choose *Tupaiia* (tree shrews)? Why? Why? Why? Endlessly, again and again. Why did natural selection choose *Primates* and then within that very same paradigm escalate to humanity? Why did this evolutionary process not take an alternate route devised for another kind of survivable creature, say from some small remnant herbivorous dinosaur, an ultimate continued survivor from the end of a tumultuous Cretaceous Period (from what is referred to as the K/T boundary extinctions)?[4]

Reiteratively, and while we're still within the speculative realm of streams of why-questions and selective variability, now why, really, lastly, why then did humanity not come to resemble some other mammalian creature such as a life form from the Order of *Cetacea* (dolphins, porpoises, and whales)? Marino, an evolutionary anthropologist, in a comparative study on the encephalization quotient levels (EQs) between the primate and odontocete (dolphin and whale) families, presents an insightful analysis where it is asserted that odontocetes (dolphins in particular) display human intelligence affinities. Marino points out that "[t]he presence of nonprimate EQs that are much closer to that of humans than the EQs of any other primate indicates that similar levels of encephalization can emerge in very different phylogenetic lineages."[5] Dolphins obtained their EQ levels within a 15 million year time period and from this it is clear that "as recently as 2.0 m.y.a. the most highly encephalized mammals to have evolved were not hominids but dolphins."[6]

And yet, of course, Marino's thesis confers an accrual of further why-questions (which I will leave here unmentioned) concerning scientific notions on selective processes and scientific regard for evolutionary transformational adaptive stasis. In consideration of Marino's analytical and comparative models, we can add that science has allowed for multiple paradigm speculations and narrative fictions on just how long it would take any other opportunistic creature to similarly evolve as *Primates* have.

Conclusively, scientific research has presented the idea that cetaceans have possessed their big brains for a much larger period than humans have and we are informed that the mystery really lies in humanity's rapid rates of increases.[7] Humanity, it seems, is quite fortunate and under such evolutionary and environmental ongoing circumstances still remains changeable. Presently, we are a faster self-regulating existential form that prospectively responds to its own surrounding and environmental disruptions; in post-postmodernity and amidst inter-human technological dependencies it seems that humanity now almost precepts impediments with its own self-initiated and self-creative biologic changes to adapt, for example, to aging and to dysfunctional organs. The unceasing rapid technological advancement will eventually lead us to discover more efficient ways to make human biophysical amendments that will correspond to climatic and environmental human affective changes.[8] It seems that there is great power in the use of brains, and the human brain is forever working at its own survival and perpetuity.

Brain usage is a very important aspect for any species, and according to a biological anthropologist, a specialist on brain development, named John M. Allman, cell brains can even be found in *E. coli*. Allman also points out that there are proto levels of brain function in a great many small minute organisms. One critical aspect of brain development according to Allman is mutational and genetic productive mechanisms that have functioned throughout the ages and throughout various species in a homologous fashion.[9] Nevertheless, it seems that size does complicate matters most in brain development because of the energy needs. According to Allman,

> Animals with large brains are rare—there are tremendous costs associated with large brains. The brains must compete with other organs in the body for the limited amount of energy available, which is a powerful constraint on evolution of large brains. Large brains also require a long time to mature, which greatly reduces the rate at which their possessors can reproduce.[10]

There is also the endless competition for metabolic energy between the gut and brain.[11] Humanity must consider itself quite fortunate because it is the prime leader and winner in balancing this struggle in which Dean Falk, another biological anthropologist, refers to as the "braindance" affair, which has become quite useful in advancing humanity.[12] As the brain complexity and size grew, so too did fortunate humanity work at a more effective implementation of the brain in order to survive with existing thought processes. Humanity must be blessed because its brain development has surpassed all other creatures. How miraculous it seems that humanity remains unique in this sole respect with its superbly enlarged neocortex. Again, one must wonder why.

Unfortunately, for the black the brain has not contended enough. In making an assessment about human brain size differentials, Rushton, a "London trained" British psychologist, points out that "Mongoloids" and "Caucasoids" have the biggest brains.[13] Rushton, in keeping with Western tradition, surveys various scientific studies and reports and makes use of them for his own "racial" assertions. When we read Rushton we encounter innovative skill in making informational-filled statements about human "racial" differences. As he reviews the data and sources he wants to project astonishment and he ends one passage by stating, "The Mongoloid-Negroid difference in brain size across so many estimation procedures is striking."[14] It seems that what is truthfully "striking" is Rushton's indirect and discrete fashion of stressing the *Caucasoid-Negroid* differences, and the *Caucasoid-Mongoloid* similarities.

Rushton uses sources like John R. Baker the late Oxford cytologist or molecular geneticist whose last bit of work back in 1974 titled *Race* turned to "racial" analysis. Baker's expertise helped to galvanize support for a scientific solution to the ethnic question and helped to validate certain perceptions concerning differing "racial" abilities. Rushton uses John R. Baker to tell us that others have noted other "racial" differences; Baker's work is presented as information of a civilizational level where the black is perceived as being noncivilizational.[15] Rushton remains consistent in his quest to unveil the elements of his perspective on black. Rushton's Western explanation of "racial" brain differentials leads him to draw a frightful conclusion about a harrowing black: "One ominous feature is Africa's inability to control its population growth, currently at 3.2% a year... If these trends continue, Africa will constitute more than a quarter of the human race by late in the next century and for a long time thereafter."[16] Beware—the black is coming to get you. So be afraid. Be very, very afraid. It seems that the small brain-sized black will someday rule the world and the white and the yellow, the supposed great contributors to human civilization, will be outcompeted and we can infer from Rushton's book that the end of civilization will surely be at hand.

Rushton continues his superb Western presentation of data and sources and he points out that black and white difference in IQ tests stand at about 15 points apart.[17] It seems that according to Rushton what holds blacks down with low IQs is "peer denigration of educational achievement."[18] But wait... there is some hope. A fortunate circumstance for the black is that they reside in the United States where it turns out that all "races" averaged larger brains than in their home continents and we are informed that the gain was largest for Africans, a whopping 92cm3, and in second place was the Asians with 54cm3 and of course last was the whites with 36cm3.[19] I suppose that the large-brained whites are not in need of much growth since they already have naturally endowed large brains. It is interesting to note that the whites are presented as just whites and the Africans encompass all the blacks who by the way trail and who are in desperate need of the mentioned growth, and of course there are the Asians which would mean the yellows who are in need of some slight gain but who are still doing just fine as they hang in second. Nonetheless, the yellows and the whites are *paulo post futurum* doomed consequentially because of those darn black social tendencies; Rushton informs us that the staggering AIDS rates in black countries are due to "perhaps" because of black sexual avariceness.[20] Uhhmmm... this sounds very familiar... Perhaps one could say it sounds Gobineau-esque.

It seems that Rushton's methodical research is in keeping with the same old kind of persevering Western thinking, and we can add that the modern West propounds the old traditional presumptions with useful and infused data to further back up (re)creative perceptions and to rightfully make it all seem so sound and validated. It seems that in brain assessments we find some that will keep holding on to that old "chain of being" that old hierarchical thought that had commenced back in the seventeenth century and that gave way to a relationship of separatist and "racialized" human beings.[21] And just as the old seventeenth century world had a social scale or class or order, so too over three hundred years later do we continue to find visions of humanity that are presented for both the black and the white.[22] We still find a Western sense of knowledge that in particular tends to construct "Africans and Native Americans" as the bridge between "European man" and creatures.[23]

NOTES

1. See Lovejoy p.183 who points out that the conception of a universe as a "chain of being," that is to say ideas about multiple living entities and their "plenitude, continuity, gradation," also infers an interconnectedness inclusive of humanity and such thoughts about humanity and nature also found its widest acceptance and spread in the eighteenth century.
2. See Jones, et al p. 199. Or see Kurten p. 2 (A Swede) who believes that Linnaeus understood and named them Primates because it meant "master animals" which is what all scholars in Linnaeus' time believed, that is to say that the categorized animals were considered physically similar to humans although it was also religiously and universally believed that they had been created independently of each other and unchangeable.
3. See Hodgen, p. 380, who asserts that throughout the seventeenth through to the nineteenth centuries A.D. scholarly notions of the "unimprovabilty of savagery" persevered and helped to justify colonization and black slavery. I would further argue that the Linnaean taxonomical categorization of humanity initialized Western perceptions of the savage as separate, half-human and black. See Hodgen, p. 434–35, who also informs us that Linnaeus ranked humans and accepted them as separate and fixed. I would further add that the Linnaean model had helped to traditionalize a separateness that had seemed well-ordered and thanks to Linnaeus and other subsequent common Western presumptions of the black, we have a base for the troubling human partings that still remain to this day.
4. See Rich p. 484, an illustration where we have a hypothetical characterization of a bipedal human sized "dinosauroid," the idea was borrowed by Rich from Dale Russell.
5. P. 83.
6. *Ibid.*
7. See also Stephan et al. (p. 25) who points out that "variation and relative size of entire brain among different mammalian orders such as *Insectivora*, *Chiroptera* and *Primates* are paralleled by morphological physiological, and behavior characteristics that, in turn, are related to environmental features." And thus, it is asserted that climatic factors are what make all the difference in the world and are what specifically helped to precipitate the primate evolution.
8. See Dixon.
9. P. 49.
10. *Ibid.*, p. 13.
11. *Ibid.*, p. 59.
12. Falk p.175. Also, Falk *passim* points out that brain "laterlization" cerebral cortex become more intricate as human developments of language and speech in particular increased.
13. See p. 4.
14. *Ibid.*, p. 133.
15. *Ibid.*, p. 142.
16. *Ibid.*, p. 161.
17. *Ibid.*, p. 138.
18. *Ibid.*, p. 279.
19. *Ibid.*, p. 283–284.
20. *Ibid.*, p. 289.
21. See Hodgen, p. 397.
22. *Ibid.*, p. 403.
23. *Ibid.*, p. 414.

Chapter Five

Global Time

GEOLOGIC CHRONOLOGIZATION

Geologists, physicists, and chemists have helped to organize the underground sedimentary levels of earth into a chronologically successive and interpretative geological construction about rock formations that have become distinctly time based and insightfully decipherable and that specifically denotes past fossilized sequences. Again, science has found order from formerly undetectable rocks. It seems that rocks have recorded stories to tell about our planet; rocks have moved and have been shaped and reshaped and are still being shaped as time moves onward.

The ascertainable geologic time-levels or scales have helped us to understand life's overall existence on planet earth. The original time boundaries that were worked out by the 1850s had been revised and now also include radiometric time-scales, which supposedly add better precision to what would be otherwise commonly referred to as "absolute dating." The two terms used, "geochronologic" and "radiometric" time-scales refer to pre-1850s and post-1850s, they can be seen as an older relative time and a more recent time classification.[1] It is very important to obtain more precise quantitative values from the principles of radioactive decay specifically for the geological periods because the long past micro-organisms and animals that existed at some recondite ancient moment in time needed better and essential and corroborating proof of past existences. The hidden dead life-forms soon became revealed and decipherable within a recognized aging earth that also became better understood and precisely dated as science continued to work at solving how life came to be or better yet humanity came to be.

In order to explain the early primate forms of life we must first understand the geologic time succession in which prehumanity existed. Let me

Figure 5.1. Earth's Age in Eons. This depiction was created by the author.

begin with a simplistic break down of key geological and chronological terms used for dividing up earth's past time-sequences. The longest period of time is an "eon" which comes from the Latin form *aeon*, which comes from the Greek *aion,* and which means, "age," or "a life period of time." Quantitatively an "eon" equals one billion years (see Figure 5.1). The next longest period of time is an "era." Mammalian creatures prop up extensively during what is called the Cenozoic era. An "era" is a specific break down used that signifies erathem. The term "era" comes from the Latin word *aer* and the word "era" itself directly comes from the Latin neuter plural form of *aer*, which is *aera* (i.e, ae + ra = e + ra) and which in Latin means "copper, brass or money." Back in the ancient Roman times the word meant a mark like a monetary mark or marker and just as it is used in Latin so too does its geologic meaning figuratively refer to a mark or marks throughout time, it is sort of similarly used to make note of or mark the three "eras" of the geological time of animal life (see Figure 5.2).

Chronologically primate evolution begins in the fossil record within the Cenozoic era and more specifically during the Cambrian period. A "period" is used to further break down an era into segments. In general, "periods" work as a subdivision of an era and "periods" are divided into two main parts: (1) the Precambrian and (2) the Cambrian groups. There are twelve periods that come after the Precambrian group and that begin with the Cambrian period. The Cambrian period is an important period because that is when animal life is believed to actually begin. All the periods relate and refer to the geologic rocks that have been formed throughout time (see Figure 5.3).

In this enquiry, the important area of focus will be the Cenozoic era. The word Cenozoic comes from a combination of two roots, the first "ceno" which means "recent" stems from the Greek word *koinos* meaning common, new, or recent, and the second is "zoic" which comes from the Greek word *zoon* or in neuter plural *zoa* which means animal or animals. The term Cenozoic era literally translates to mean "the recent era of animals" and this part of geologic history is divided into two periods, the Tertiary and the Quaternary periods --rather both periods add up to over a 65 million year span of time--both periods are significant because anthropoid transformational development has been respectively inferred as occurring within these two periods (see Figure 5.4). Our geologically proven prehistoric time-sequences required that the Tertiary period (ranging from 65 m.y.a. to 2 m.y.a.) be organized into two major parts, that is the specific geologic terms of the Early Tertiary (or the Paleogene) and the Late Tertiary (or the Neogene) (again, see Figure 5.4). The Paleogene and the Neogene came from the Greek prefixes *paleo* "old" and *neo* "new" combined with the root word *gene*, which comes from the Greek verb *genethai* meaning "to be born" such as an inference of the time when *anthropos* was born and of when its descent begins. Throughout these prehistoric times a great many primatological developments had transpired and so throughout the Tertiary and Quaternary periods a more timed specificity was required.

Epochs are a further break down within the Tertiary and Quaternary periods, the term "epoch" derived from Latin *epocha,* which further also stems from Greek *epoche* and which finally means "cessation," or "fixed point in time." Also, when we review epochs we encounter again the word "cene."

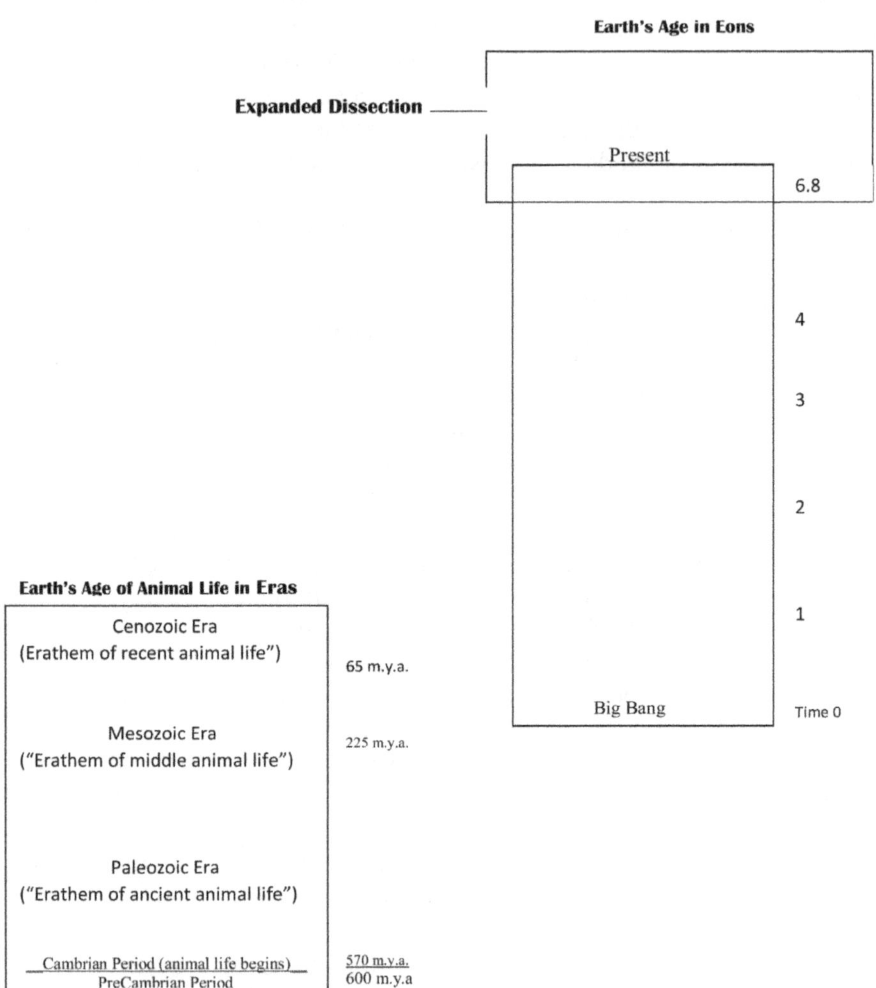

Figure 5.2. Earth's Age of Animal Life in Eras. This depiction was created by the author.

Once again the Latin derivative of "cene" *koinos* is used, as with the Cenozoic era, and it is used in regards to epochs in a somewhat redundant sense. Moreover, for example the Paleocene epoch, which occurs under the Cenozoic era, can literally mean "the old [cene = 'recent'] epoch" and again within the Cenozoic era, which translates to "the recent era of animals." The Paleocene epoch in the Cenozoic era would somewhat confusedly and literally mean the "old-recent epoch" in the "recent era of animals," and thus it is

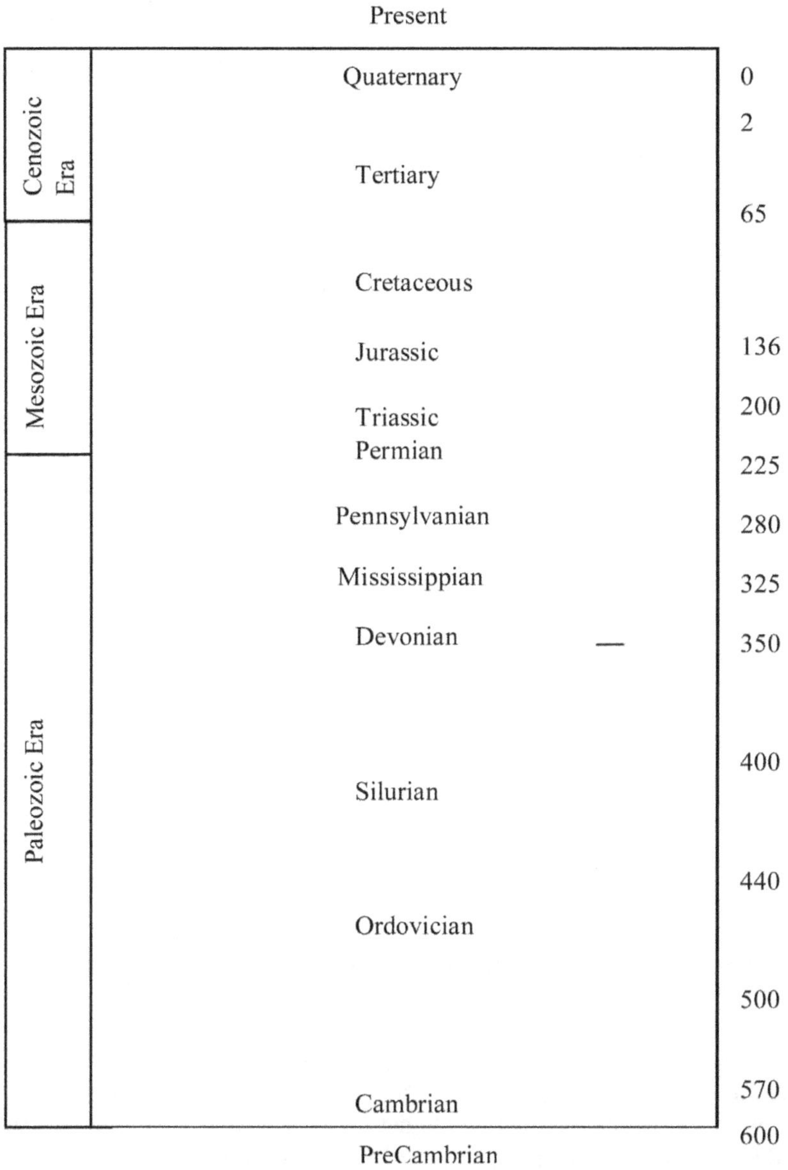

Present

Era	Period	Millions of years
Cenozoic Era	Quaternary	0
		2
	Tertiary	
		65
Mesozoic Era	Cretaceous	
	Jurassic	136
	Triassic	200
Paleozoic Era	Permian	225
	Pennsylvanian	280
	Mississippian	325
	Devonian	350
		400
	Silurian	
		440
	Ordovician	
		500
		570
	Cambrian	600

PreCambrian

Figure 5.3. Earth's Age in Periods after Pre-Cambrian. This depiction was created by the author.

the oldest epoch and in sequential order the first epoch to commence under the Cenozoic era (see Figure 5.5).

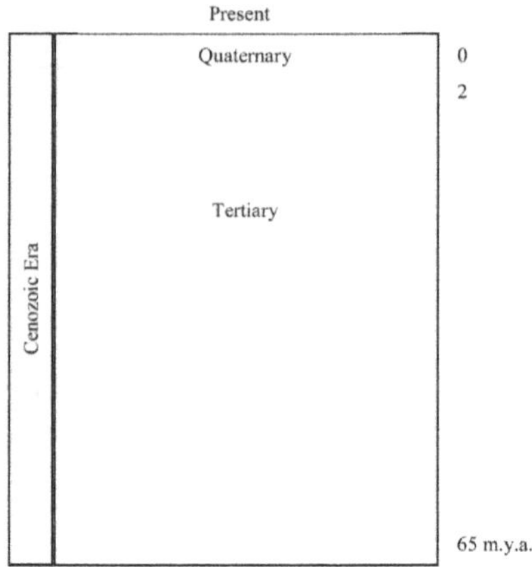

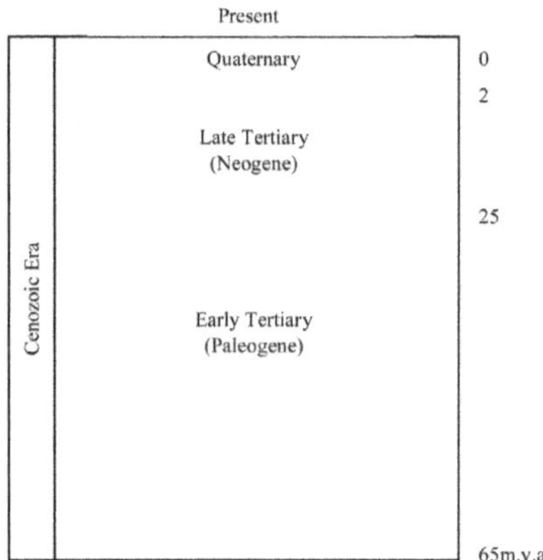

Figure 5.4. Earth's Two Most Recent Periods. This depiction was created by the author.

Geology came up with the term "epoch" as a time-based sign created to assist in the further respective segmentation of our planet's long natural history. In the 1830s a British geologist by the name of Charles Lyell subdivided the Tertiary period (65 m.y.a. to 2 m.y.a.) into three epochs, the Eocene (65 m.y.a. to 25 m.y.a.), the Miocene (25 m.y.a. to 5 m.y.a.), and the Pliocene (5 m.y.a. to 2 m.y.a.). It seems that all good subdivisions must originally come in threes, in trinary, or better yet in Trinitarian fashion just as with the Stone, Bronze and Iron ages. In regard to the epochs the oldest was initially called the (1) Eocene (that is why it received the title *eo* meaning "dawn" with again the root word *cene* meaning "new" or "recent," the (2) Miocene

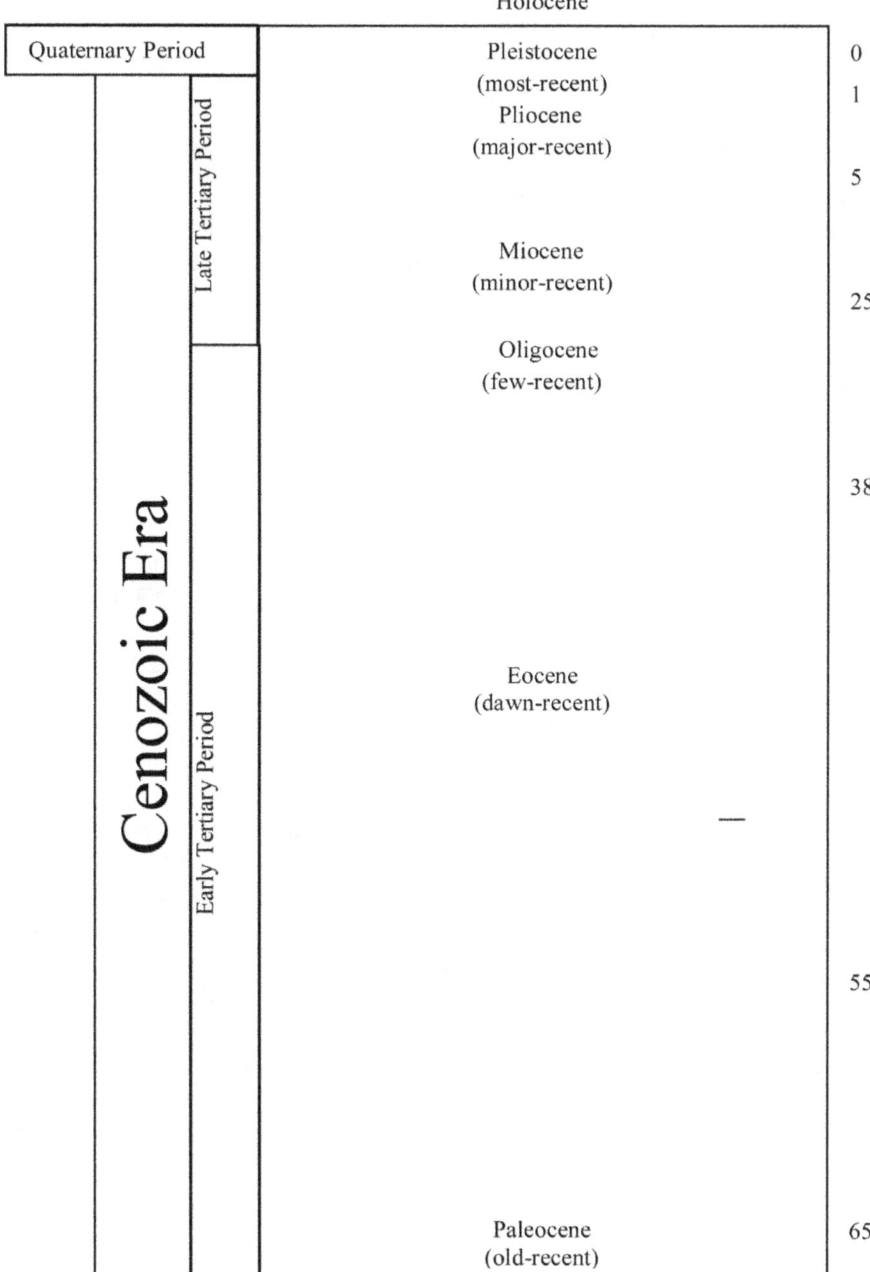

Figure 5.5. Earth's Age in Recent Epochs. This depiction was created by the author.

(meaning "minor-recent" for it was minor in events) and the (3) Pliocene (meaning "major-recent" for it was major in events) (again, see Figure 5.5).

Subsequently, referenced changes occur, the Pliocene no longer became the last epoch as the Pleistocene now succeeds it. The Pliocene and the Pleistocene, older and newer halves: the Pliocene is considered the "major-recent" and the Pleistocene is considered the "most-recent" or newer where "pleisto" comes from the Greek word *pleistos* meaning "most." Also, please note that sometimes they are combined and are referred to as the Plio-Pleistocene, which comparatively speaking displays a short time span. The Plio-Pleistocene contained a great many archaic life-form activity and its closeness is held due to the inundating fossil remains discovered throughout what has been perceived as a closely linked prehistoric time span. Finally, the last epoch is the present geologic period, which begins at 10,000 years ago and is referred to as the Holocene (meaning "whole-recent").[2]

Extensive fossil remains and data accrued within the early part of the twentieth century and modern science had become more technologized and now required greater precision, the 1960s found a need for progressively more subdivided geologic time-sequences and more useful specificity, as the archaeological record grew more expansive with more time-partitionalized fossils.[3] Thus, new epochs were added, the Paleocene epoch ("old-recent epoch") was placed between the pre-existing Cretaceous period and the once dawn of time Eocene ("dawn-recent") epoch. Also, the added Paleocene epoch now becomes the oldest (hence the name *paleo* which again literally means "old"). Another addition was made with the Oligocene ("few-recent") epoch because of its short duration, which is placed between the Eocene ("dawn-recent") and Miocene ("minor-recent") epochs. And so, the final order of epochs becomes, Paleocene, Eocene, Oligocene, Miocene, Pliocene, Pleistocene, and lastly the present Holocene. (again, see Figure 5.5).

One could say that these amendments occurred in the middle of the twentieth century because again it wasn't until the 1960s that a more respective and interpretative and self-correcting science required punctilious breakdowns as thematic and groupable anthropoid life-form fossils began to be formulated via an ascertaining archaeology. Science, particularly paleontology, geology, physical anthropology, and archaeology, required validate-able *in situ* proveniences of a past that had formerly remained quite contestable, that is until a scientific modernity came along with its strong and powerful technological and geo-analytical devices to interpret where fossils laid amidst rocks and thus now quantifiably within a more obtainable and revealing time-sequenced prehistoric past.

BLACK GONDWANALAND

Let us for the moment turn to the great geologic formulation of what I will call a post-Pang*aea* world. As humanity remains unique we must also note that so too is our precious earth. We must also keep in mind that as humanity has formed and is still forming into what will inevitably come so too has our inimitable planet earth changed and so too will our special planet earth come to encounter further changes. Change is an inevitable constant occurrence. And now throughout the changes that have occurred, and that are still occurring, one thing apparently remained the center of all things. I will propose here and now that the center of the world had always been Africa. And thus in a logistic sense as we discover that the great African continent had been better yet the metacenter of what has been described as formerly a supercontinent I will point out that our great African center (traditionally portrayed as the heart of what a white *creatrix* has perceived as an abominable darkness) is the center of us all. We are all black derived as the center of the world can be said to be an Africanic based Pang*aea* (see Figure 5.6).

Our world was once quite united and it has been viewed as uniformly one large entity. There have been postulations into just how united and connected our world had once been and subsequently it was called *Pangaea,* which literally means "an *all-combined* earth," *Gaea* is the Greek word for land and the goddess of the Earth. There were other terms that were thought of such as the term used back in 1931 by a Henry Smith Williams who perceived the world's unity and addressed it as "The First Continent."[4] There can be no doubt that complete wholeness and a seamless beginning was an essential part of our origin. We should always be reminded of this and never forget that we all came from an Earth that had once been one indistinguishable land mass.

When we look at how the world first began we must consider Gondwanaland or better yet the greatest part of Pangaea called Gondwana and or what I will call black Gondwana for its center ultimately became today's African continent. The centerpiece of Pangaea has been called Gondwana and the African continent is its central remnant. Rock analyzations deep into earth's crust have proven an integral connection in particular between South Africa and India. Gondwanaland or the forest of Gond, which is named after a place located in central India, was a critical piece of geographic land area.

The prehistoric Gondwanaland was a supercontinent, which included, first and foremost, Africa, and South America, the peninsular India, Australia, and Antarctica. The name came from the famous Austrian geologist named Eduard Suess when he noted that the Upper Paleozoic era and Mesozoic era rock formations in various geographic locations like that of South Africa and India had shared geologic features that could be found in all the listed geographic areas, i.e. Africa, South America, India, Australia, and

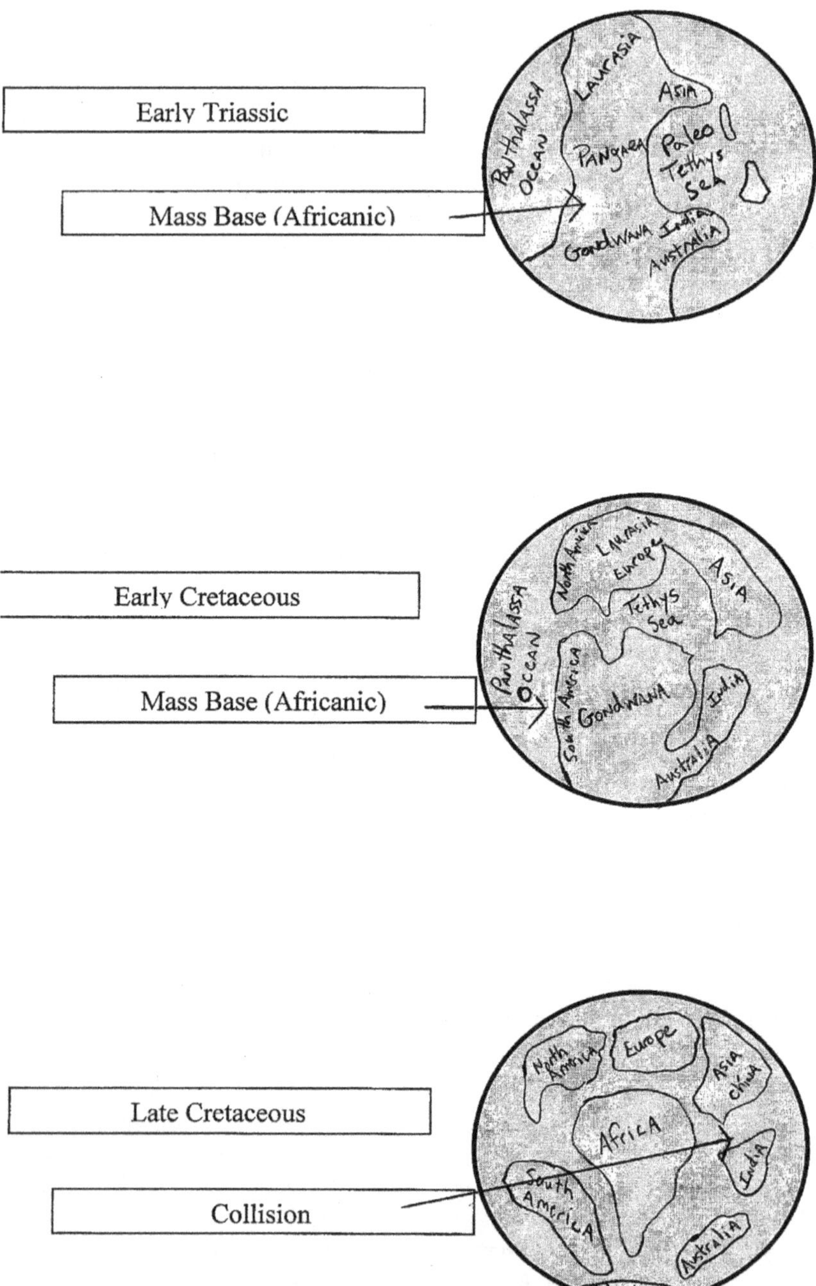

Figure 5.6. Cretaceous, Triassic, and the Pre-Africanic. This depiction was created by the author.

Antarctica. The geologic evidence that proves the connection between the various locations and that displays rock strata similarities are called the Karoo System in South Africa, the Gondwana System in India, and the Santa Catarina System in South America.[5] Similarities in particular date from the Permian period that existed well over 250 million years ago and the fact that we find similar plants and faunas in the mentioned geographic areas also had helped science to come to the conclusion of a former consummated origin (again, see Figure 5.3).

Alexander Du Toit, a South African geologist from Johannesburg, wrote a book, which had been dedicated to the famous German meteorologist Alfred Wegener entitled *Our Wandering Continents*: *An Hypothesis of Continental Drifting* dated in 1937 and he proposed a place called Laurasia. Since the 1930s it was a commonly held scientific belief that during the Mesozoic era between roughly around 250 m.y.a and 66 m.y.a. the Tethys Ocean became a Sea as it intrusively separated the two supercontinents of Gondwanaland from Laurasia. The critical break up began back at around 250 m.y.a. during the middle Permian period when the rifting of what was called the Tethys Sea first occurred. Science believes that various geologic activity helped cause the supercontinent Gondwana to separate from Laurasia the other supercontinent (again, see Figure 5.6).

The Laurasia continental mass once located in the Northern Hemisphere included North America, Europe, and Asia except for the peninsular India which we now know was once part of Gondwana and is currently pushing its way underneath Asia (see again Figure 5.6). It seems that rifts are part of earth's fervent existence and will continue to occur and to cause further terrestrial disruptions. We must accept the fact that geologic metamorphism, volcanic and tectonic activities are always occurring all throughout the world and such fragmentations will remain part of our earthly existence.

With the shifting of tectonic plates, at about 175 m.y.a Gondwanaland began to break up, and the Indian fragment, carried by what has been called the Indian-Australian plate, began to drift slowly northward toward the much larger Eurasian plate (again, see Figure 5.6). Ultimately, the Indian-Australian plate breaks apart as well. Gondwanland's dispersion from that time and throughout many of millions of years gradually worked at moving into today's position. India finally collided (at approximately 50 m.y.a.), the northern edge of what once had been the Indian-Austrian plate was thrust under at a low angle at what once had been the Eurasian plate.

Today India is still forcing its way into Asia, which is causing what is called an underthrusting, or subduction. The geologic term for the plate activity called subduction actually means that one lithospheric plate (land base) is being led underneath another lithospheric plate as two land bases or plates meet head on in a region described as a convergent boundary. The colliding pieces of land inevitably lead to building a thicker land base and a union of what once had been separated pieces of land, and the piece of land or plate that is driving into a continent sinks underneath the continent and melts away into what is called the earth's asthenosphere. The effects of this landmass collision throughout a convergent zone in what has formed much of the Himalayan mountain range and Tibetan Plateau and is what is called diastrophism, which we find today in the Indian or rather Asian region.

It seems that as time had moved forward our planet earth became affected by several geologic activities such as orogenic deformation (thick crust mountain belt transformation), magnetism, and in general land metamorphism, which particularly has had a profound effect significantly ever since the Permian period. Just what causes such visceral disruptions like those in the Permian period remains somewhat still speculative. Others would differ and argue that it had all been due to a specific cataclysmic event, which caused the Gondwanaland supercontinent to separate from the Lauriasia supercontinent as the Paleo Tethys Sea made its way through the supercontinents. Some believe that it had been primarily a catastrophic event that helped precipitate intense thrust faulting as continual earthly activity of granitic and andesitic magnetism and high temperatures, and low-pressure metamorphism worked its rifting magic between Gondwana and Laurasia.

We recently learned of the magnanimous powers of rifting and it wasn't until especially the 1960s that science was able to note evidence of the seafloor spreading from the loci of oceanic ridges, which helped to further prove that the ocean basins were not permanent global features. Hence, worldwide our earth is forever in the midst of changing, and the frightening occurrence of continental drift have helped to keep various geographic locations continuously transforming and it is believed that it is all due to the inner-earth motion that is always going on. The molten heat that remains deep down below the earth's crust will continue to affect our planet and yet unfortunately the all mighty heat that has helped to shape our world and in a sense has also helped to create what we have become will also one day come to cool down and irretrievably end.

A CLIMATIC PALEOCENE

All the land changes that have gone on throughout time have also come to affect in particular struggling animal life forms that existed throughout and on top of a very malleable earth's crust. By the end of the Cretaceous period and the beginning of the Paleocene epoch the infamous mass extinction of dinosaurs comes to a close. By the beginning of the Paleocene epoch the gruesome mass extinction of dinosaurs brings to a tragic conclusion the reign of a once superior and invincible life form. The end of the Cretaceous period is now commonly referred to as the K/T boundary where it is believed that a cataclysmic event supposedly occurred in one moment (or perhaps a long extended moment in time). It seems that a profound geologic event transpired around about 65 m.y.a. between the end of the Cretaceous period (K) and the beginning of the Early Tertiary period (T), hence the acronym "K/T." The event perhaps spans as little as 10 years or even 3 months or perhaps several thousands of years as science still does not precisely know how long the catastrophe took place. It seems that the geologic evidence for some kind of intense climatic disruptions during the K/T boundary may have been the primary cause for the wiping away of large life forms almost in their entirety. The specific unfortunate catastrophic event had supposedly wiped out about 76% of the world's life forms. What occurred at the K/T boundary will perhaps not be the last of worldwide living disruptions for paleontologists have now come to attribute earth's long existence with various cyclic to processual global mass extinctions.

Unfortunately, the last great paroxysmal intrusion of our continuously changing and developing world and at most times harmonious existence had by the beginning of the Early Tertiary period (65 m.y.a.) come to just settle for the moment. More specifically by this time when we arrive at the Paleocene epoch the termination of old occasions brought forth a renewal and a rebirth of what can be considered a reinvigorated brave new world. Throughout such precarious and still yet animal inhabited times the Paleocene prosimians began quite small and as time continued they begin to develop stronger teeth and various other physical attributes.

Again, tree shrews and in general prosimians were quite multiple and as striving speciation takes its course these early primates were making use of all kinds of variegated physical characteristics. They develop stronger teeth and jaws for grinding and limb and eye changes made life for these once small and lightweight creatures more survivable and persistent. Prosimians are considered animals such as lemurs, lorises, and tarsiers, which now can only be found in tropical regions like those of South America. One can suspect that a tropical climate was probably the kind of climate that was needed for the fruition of these kinds of prosimians back in the Paleocene epoch almost 60 m.y.a.

The prosimians reach a peak back at around 60 m.y.a. and they prosper in the world for a very long period with again appearances and disappearances of variant forms, but then geographical and environmental changes start to occur and by the time we arrive at the early Oligocene epoch 38 m.y.a. other essential persisting life form changes take place. What happens between 60–38 m.y.a. as it concerns the fundamental and progressive development of little tree shrews and prosimians still requires further research. Science has not explained or has not found much throughout these transpired millions of years.

NOTES

1. See Considine, p. 1431–1432.
2. The first two syllables of the word "Holo"comes from *holos,* the Greek word which means "whole or complete." Charles Lyell had chosen Holocene to refer to the "entirely modern" embedded fossils as to contrast it with the "mostly new," which again is the word that refers to the (pleisto" and "cene") Pleistocene strata, see Tattersall (1988) p. 245.
3. Simons (1972) p.11 solely points out that time changes did not occur until the 1960's.
4. See Williams p. 3.
5. See King p. 309–11.

Chapter Six

My Dear Little "Negrillo" Looking Tree Shrew

I would like to focus for the moment on the little tree shrew, the little creature that Western science, particularly paleoprimatology, has considered foremost and preliminary. Little tree shrews have come to be viewed as the notable *prima facie* model form of the preprimate evolutionary antepenult or rather as the grandiose debutante little quadrapod, the premiere form, or even the "antecedent of man" as the phrase was used in a title of a book on primates by the infamous Sir Wilfred Le Gros Clark back in 1978. Let us consider the last sentence in an article by a reputable source and specialist R. D. Martin who comments about how differing, in a general living spectrum, tree shrew mothers are because they spend such a short period of time nursling. Tree shrews seem to be chastised for not being humanly caring enough. Martin concludes his overall summary of the species by saying, "For my part, I am inclined to believe that tree shrew mothers have simply hit upon an extremely economical way of avoiding the maternal burdens carried by other mammals, most notably by the primates, including the human female."[1] It is commonly assumed that this small mammalian creature can be compared, and, in a sense, becomes in a simplistic level an analogue of prehumanity.

Tree shrews or the formulated Latin term *Tupaiia* or *Tupaiiadae* (the latter word refers to the entire family) are very important creatures when we try to envision what archaic tree shrews must have looked like. In a general encyclopedia we are told that the term *tupaiia* comes from an English naturalist by the name of Sir Thomas Stamford Raffles who back in 1821 classified the *tupayas* as insectivores and who coined the scientific generic name *Tupaia* from the Malay word for squirrel "*tupai.*"[2] A Malay word, a term from the Malay, a culture that would easily be considered nonwhite, hence a black cultural term had been used. It was the renown former President of the

Royal Society and formerly Darwin's pit bulldog and great defender of evolutionism, Thomas Henry Huxley, who back in 1872 first headed attention to these little squirrel-like creatures when he noted similarities between tree shrews and monkeys.[3] And it was the Yale trained great American paleontologist and zoologist, George Gaylord Simpson, who went on further in 1945 and classified them as prosimians.[4] The term *prosimian* comes from the prefix "pro" meaning "before" and the Latin root word "*simia*" meaning "ape," and thus prosimians are considered that which came "before ape." Back in the 1940s and up through to the 1970s tree shrews garnered a pinnacle point of attention as the times before that, a time-span of about forty years, the scientific creativities were primarily more concerned with larger primate forms. Visions of precursory and prehuman small mammalian creatures had been too fanciful and therefore were not of such great concern. The supposedly small analogue with clearly notable physiological remnant features of an embryonic form of prehumanity existed throughout an analyzable prehistoric past and had soon attracted some scientific interest as a modern synthesis was being thoroughly established. Unfortunately, tree shrews are still seen as somewhat too preliminary and they have been kept on the sidelines as there has not been much of field and laboratory devotion.

There has been as of recent some phylogenetic reconstructing and at the scientific physiological level it has been consistently noted that tree shrews have definitely certain combined anatomical traits with especially proto-developmental primates. Nonetheless, they also have been given their own equal footing as *Scandentia* within their own Order since comparative biologists still cannot precisely explain these small mammalian creatures as belonging to either *Primates* or *Insectivora*. Again, it was the great defender of Primates overall and their link to humans, Sir Le Gros Clark former head of the department of human anatomy at Oxford who first argued that tree-shrews should be seen as belonging to Primates.

Scientifically primate evolutionary origin is believed to have begun with early and small pervasive mammalian creatures that soon began to thrive worldwide. There are diverse forms of prehistoric mammals, but paleoanthropology has defined specifically some kind of small and *Tupaiian*-like form as the pre-eminent precursory creature that tended toward elementary primatological characteristics and that led the way to anthropoid beginnings. As science continues to solely rationalize and we have not yet obtained in the fossil record an archaic *Tupaiia* of any sort, it seems that a very long time ago over 65 million years ago it is scientifically present that a small *Tupaiian*-like creature persists and in a way inherits the earth. By around the end of the Cretaceous period, after the K/T boundary extinctions (again, K/T stands for an agreed upon point in time that lies somewhere between the end of the Cretaceous (K) and the beginning of the Tertiary (T) periods dating to around 65 million years ago) an environmental and ecological beneficence was rendered to a small placental mammalian creature. Soon after the mass extinction of dinosaurs around the beginning of the Tertiary period (or Paleocene epoch) small and very fortunate *Tupaiian*-like creatures abide by the so-called and ever-so-progressive forces of natural selection.

It is believed that as time moved forward *Tupaiian*-like forms soon gave way to larger growing creatures. Despite the fact that fossil remains from the early Paleocene remain sketchy and quite indecisive, from analyzations mostly of the teeth remains, it is believed that early primate forms like for example the ones from the families of *Plesiadapidae* and *Paromomyidae* (both prosimians) have been discovered in the Paleocene and Eocene epochs of Europe and North America and they are what Western science begins to access as morphological progression by, for example, reformulations in dentition. There are forms that have been discovered and that fall within the Primates Order and in comparison they come to the next developmental level and as to what would come after something of a tree shrew.[5]

Western science has gone on to describe prehumanity's ascent not only at a very prime level from fish, but also from a little mammalian creature, a little tree shrew. Sir Le Gros Clark, the great marketer of tree shrews who put them on the map of primate desendency, cautioned about fanciful comparative modeling such as that made by analyzations of *Tupaiia* and resembling prehistoric fossilized specimens, but then he himself begins his story on the origins of *Primates* with

> We may now picture the emergence of the Primates in the Paleocene (or more probably in the latter part of the preceding Cretaceous Period) in the form of small arboreal creatures very similar to the modern tree-shrews, alert, active and agile among the branches, relying more and more on the discriminative potentialities of the visual sense, and less and less on the more limited scope of the olfactory sense.[6]

It is believed that antecedent *Primates* development begins to take foot somehow with tree shrew-like forms (*tupaiaformes*) or rather ground dwelling squirrel-like creatures that then subsequently, as time passes on and as they maintain and persist throughout long periods of what can be viewed as stasis, moved (it is scientifically believed) from terrestrial to arboreal insectivores. Evolutionary forces press on, perhaps tree shrew-like forms endure on through a transitory passage way, and they persevere through a general multivariate life form as existentially intertwined environmental and biological complexities continue to increase. In general, with the use of primarily modern comparative anatomical analysis and theoretical modeling prehistoric extinct forms are assumed to exhibit analogical traits depicted in extant forms and a staunch Western science has assumed that the fossil forms were very similar to the presently still existing small creatures.

Archaic tree shrew-like forms were mostly considered to be prehistoric insectivores and are also interpreted to be the forerunners of primates because they ambivalently shared primitive primate-like anatomical characteristics as well as being insectivores in several respects such as with their hands and feet, which are commonly more like claws of insectivores than primates. They are considered to be a kind of transitional Order between primates and archaic insectivores. Also at one time they were even considered to be like a Lemur and hence they also became part of the *Lumeriformes*.[7]

Recently, within the last decade of the twentieth century, at the molecular level in laboratory work done on genomic features of highly repeated DNAs, molecular biological studies has found that they were not close to primates when tree shrew DNA (in particular, the common *Tupaiiadae glis*) had been hybridized with isolated DNA fragments of several non-human primates and one insectivore (*E. europaeus*). The results pointed to a consensus that tree shrews should be separated from both *Primates* and *Insectivora* and that hybridization testing on joining the various DNAs has proven that tree shrews are rightly placed in the Order of *Scandentia*.[8] Unfortunately, even with molecular analyses Western science is still in doubt about the classification of this modern day analogue. The little creature that has been considered a primal form that helped propel humanity's lines of descendants has been scaled up to a higher level. Western science has devised and miniaturized this form as a preliminary proto-form that sometimes may fall within a *Primates* classification and it should be noted here that such hypothesizations are not entirely due to molecular introspections but to various tenuous (and Western science-validated) theorizations on physiological convergences and envisioned described primate characteristic retentions.

Extant tree shrews are small and agile inhabitants presently of the forests of Southeast Asia and they mostly resemble squirrels more than they do primitive apes or primitive monkeys. The family *Tupaiidae* is divided into two subfamilies: the *Tupaiinae*, which includes five genera, and the *Ptilocercinae* having only one genus, the pen-tail tree shrew. They are all funny looking little creatures, i.e., almost cartoonish with long-snouted noses. It would seem quite comical to explain and point out to a learning child that humanity would derive from a similar outstretched-nosed little creature as a *Lyonogale tana* (see Figure 6.1).

Something like a tree shrew is believed to have been the primates' likeliest ancestor because they have certain comparative traits (i.e., on a small scale of course). Paleontologists have assessed their enlarged brain relative to body size (Encephalization Quotient), their early primate-like teeth formation, and their very preliminary opposing thumb (as it begins to display separateness from the remaining four fingers. Their hands and their feet are more insectivore-like (i.e. clawed) and their toes are not much set off.[9] And although tree shrews do not have flat nails on any digits and even retain three pairs of lower incisors that seem more comb-formed for grooming and unlike *Primates*, nonetheless, they are still considered "the most primate-like non-primates."[10]

Here we come to an attempt to understand just how divisive the white creativities can surely be. Tree-shrews are seen as the nearest thing to primates and so too tree shrews are used as an analogical human racializing comparative. The well-learned and paradoxical priest on evolution named Teilhard de Chardin had cautioned and made conclusive inferences about these little creatures which remain somewhat outside a scientific classification:

> Let us carefully consider these little animals who preserve the appearance of an animal group of very ancient expansion (doubtless not very distant, morphologically, from the Cretaceous mammals); it is they, most probably, who are the pre-Primates. At a certain moment, no animal existed on earth that was so close to humanity's path of development as the little climber.[11]

Indeed Teilhard, as most of anthropological science by the early part of the twentieth century customarily affirmed, considered that the *Tupaiidae* had been the best candidate. Teilhard went further and asserts that the present day lemurs and tarsiers are "isolated survivors." It seems that making comparisons about the early forms or preliminary forms of *Primates* is all that a paleoanthropologist has.

Figure 6.1. Tree Shrew. Excerpted from *Encyclopedia Britannica*, 1911.

Unfortunately, Teilhard did not just restrict himself to pre-*Primates*. When the sacrosanct Teilhard explains the prehistoric passage of prehumanity's initial development he reminds us of other kinds of present-day survivors. According to Teilhard, lemurs and tarsiers, considered a transitional group and an initial link to further developed forms, are identified as remnants of a lesser form of *Primates.* And as Teilhard continues on the topic of primate anatomical progression, he goes on to say that "[o]ne could say that in a more accentuated form they stand to present-day apes as Australian Aborigines and Negrillos do to the white human race."[12] That is to say, that our *Tupaiidae* present-day remnants (lemurs and tarsiers included) are to apes as Australian Aborigines and Negrillos are to "the white human race," that is to say that Australian Aborigines and Negrillos (those little near human negroes) are at a lower level of humanity, they are subhuman as Teilhard helped to scientifically categorize one *racialized* precursor after another (see Figure 6.2).

Despite all the priestly and scientific envisioning on humanity that had been inferred, Teilhard had not been creative enough to note that the real present-day disparity stemming from such biased preconceived notions helped to contribute to a systemic science that had become proscriptive on accentuating human dissimilarity. Unfortunately he failed to see universal human equality and instead joined in and added theoretical building blocks to the early twentieth century chain of dissimilar human beings and all of this despite even his draped religiosity.

When we come to look at Western scientific classificatory insistences on organizing the early stages of archaic *Primates* we must note that *Tupaiidae* is held under polyphyletic taxa positioning, that is to say that this ambivalent family is attached to both *Primates* and *Insectivora*, it is in between divided realms because it has a little of both. Also, in regards to extant forms it would be considered a similitude or a sort of remnant of a very archaic past. In regards to Teilhard's analogy specifically this meant that *Tupaiia* and Negrillos were remnants from a primitive past, both were construed as transitory life forms and this is what Teilhard meant when he refers to the "in-betweens." According to scientific anthropology in the early twentieth century blacks are believed to reside between animality and humanity. We could also perhaps further assert that Teilhard saw (figuratively) a similarity between the mannerism of the indigenous Negrillos and the characteristically noted very lively and very aggressive nature of the *Tupaiidae*. Again, both have been perceived as being closer to a chthonic nature and lower human form within a scientifically and hierarchical construct.

The artifacts, the fossils of *Tupaiidae,* have maintained significance and in a theorized sense their early twentieth century interpretive meaning adds to the greatness of the forever-partializing assumptions commonly held about humanity. For now unfortunately it is *Tupaiidae* that must recede into the

Figure 6.2. Negrillo. Originally titled "African Pygmies," this is a copy excerpted from the *Collier New Encyclopedia* Vol.1, 1921, page 58-B.

background of our analysis of progressive prehuman development for we must move on in this diachronlogical analysis. As we continue this enquiry on the significance of layers of meaning behind scientific explanation and validation of a processualized humanity, here we must be aware of the real usefulness of a further insurmountable and *racially* constructing and contributive science, a specifically destructive knowledge which had been created by a biased and a re-newly revealed anthropological science, a science that still continues on the whole to manufacture further ideological concepts on how humanity arrived to the present from a bestial and validated past. And so in this work we must proceed and further deconstruct the objectified remnants of the colossal head of past and present researchers as it regards the making of humans.

Lastly overall, according to comparative paleoanthropology as the ingredients of the making of humanity were being extrapolated it is believed that very small tree shrews changed, that is to say that they grew bigger physically and evolutionarily speaking they progressed to advanced prosimians. Tree shrews are considered to be primates' ancestors, and although they had an archaic inner ear design, they were the first to begin to use a digit that may have been somewhat opposable to the fingers. And yet there are those who would argue that tree shrews should not be added under the *Primates* parent group because they do not quite maintain a substantial portion of general primate characteristics. Somewhat still hindered, science continues its quest to answer the question of just how was it that humanity came to be sorted.

NOTES

1. Martin, p. 32.
2. Grzimek, p. 5.
3. Ibid.
4. Ibid.
5. W.E. Le Gros Clark p. 73.
6. W.E. Le Gros Clark p. 323.
7. W.E. Le Gros Clark p. 71.
8. Crovella,S. *et al.* p. 50.
9. Grzimek, p.4.
10. Simon (1972) p. 65.
11. Teilhard (1965) p. 36.
12. Teilhard (1965) p. 36.

Chapter Seven

Anthropoidal Beginnings

STRIVING ANTHROPOIDS

After the Paleocene epoch as time moves forward and the geological variations that caused significant climatic alterations occur in particular such as the cooling of the Northern regions of our planet earth, prosimians worldwide are outcompeted. It seems that better equipped monkey-like forms outnumber them. As time proceeds they enter a new ecological niche and become their very own descendants. The prosimians had a metamorphosis and helped to bring on stronger and in sense larger transformed entities as time progressed. The physical landscapes had changed which precipitated altered environments. By the time we arrive at the late Eocene and early Oligocene epochs we have the appearance of various stronger forms supposedly transitioned from prosimians now referred to as anthropoids. They are called anthropoids because this is what science asserts and they help make the evolutionary beginnings of a significant ascendancy towards *anthropos* or rather humanity.[1]

It is believed that anthropoids evolved from the descendants of the small tarsiers or lemurs (i.e. prosimians) that have been found dating back to the Paleocene epoch. Monkeys, apes, and humans all can be considered Higher Primates, and they all belong to the other Suborder of *Primates* called *Anthropoidea* (see Figure 7.1). The term *anthropoidea* comes from the combination of the Greek word *anthropos* and the Latin suffix *oidea*, which is in this instance used in the word *Anthropoidea* in the Latin neuter plural form and translate into "animals characterized by the nature of *anthropos*." It was thought that the category encompassed aspects of *anthropos* or better yet resembling humanity. Science has come to attribute the beginnings of a prehuman derivation. In the anthropoid Suborder there are two prominent kinds of Higher Primates (1) the platyrrhines and (2) the catarrhines (see Figure 7.1).

According to two paleoprimatologists considered key scholarly sources, Fleagle and Kay, platyrrhines (New World primates with flat noses) and catarrhines (Old World primates with noses turned down) have been found in the fossil record and they point out that "in the past 5 years our understanding of early anthropoid evolution has changed in two ways: through the discovery of new more primitive anthropoids from Egypt and from a diversity of early anthropoids from other localities..."[2] It is the catarrhines that become important because by the time we arrive at 40 m.y.a. these Old World anthropoids help to shape the differences that produce not only apes but also humans. Humans belong to the catarrhine group along with Old World monkeys and apes. There had been over forty different kinds of catarrhines almost half of them are now extinct. The catarrhines come in various sizes from as small as the size of squirrels to that of the great apes. A key catarrhine found in Egypt had been the *Oligopithecus* a form that was believed to be part ape and part prosimian and yet its size was that of a small monkey.[3]

One key type of Paleocene genus, which had been considered found in North America and Europe and had been somewhat archaic, i.e. known as one of the most archaic primate is the form called *Plesiadapis*. The name *Plesiadapis* actually turns out to mean *plasi*- "half way towards" the *apis* bull or "sacred bull." The term comes from "George Cuvier's misnomer for a lemur-like primate from the French Eocene, Adapis, which he thought was related to cattle."[4] The bones themselves of the archaic forms were first thought to have been those of bulls or thought to be like those found in ancient Egypt as well as ancient Crete and other ancient Near Eastern cultures that worshiped bulls. What misguided some of these great scholars was

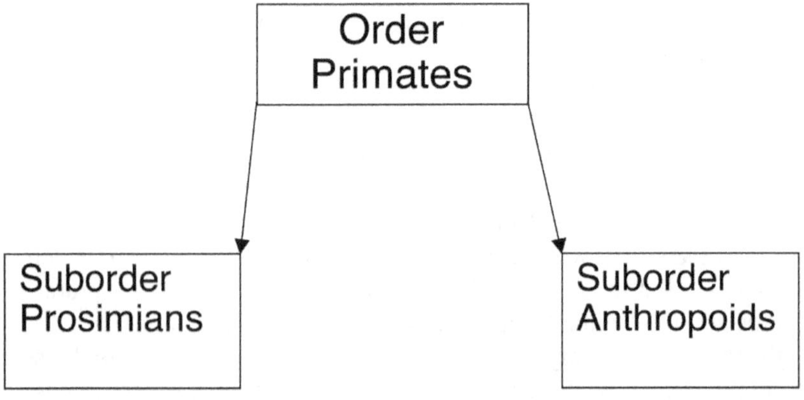

Figure 7.1. Primate Order. This depiction was created by the author.

that the skulls actually did look like those of bulls where one can easily discern the long snouts or maxillary portions of the skulls like those that also were once seen in an American Death Valley environmental motif. The plesiadapids become extinct in the Eocene epoch.

OLIGOCENE MINIMALISM

The cooler northern climates of the earth dating from the Oligocene times (38–25 m.y.a.) again contributed to the evolutionary appearances of the more ecologically efficient and developing anthropoids. The primates that were capable of withstanding the changing climatic demands and tolerated the cold helped to precipitate anthropoids. Most anthropoids wound up living longer than prosimians and most even still had tails. Early anthropoids were some really old finds of what can be considered prototypical forms that partly helped our evolutionary passage along as time continued on. Exceptionally archaic anthropoids were found in a North African region and this is quite a distance from the traditional sites of the later and more advanced primates that we traditionally find located at places like Kenya and Tanzania. The few early forms that we do find come at just the beginning of the

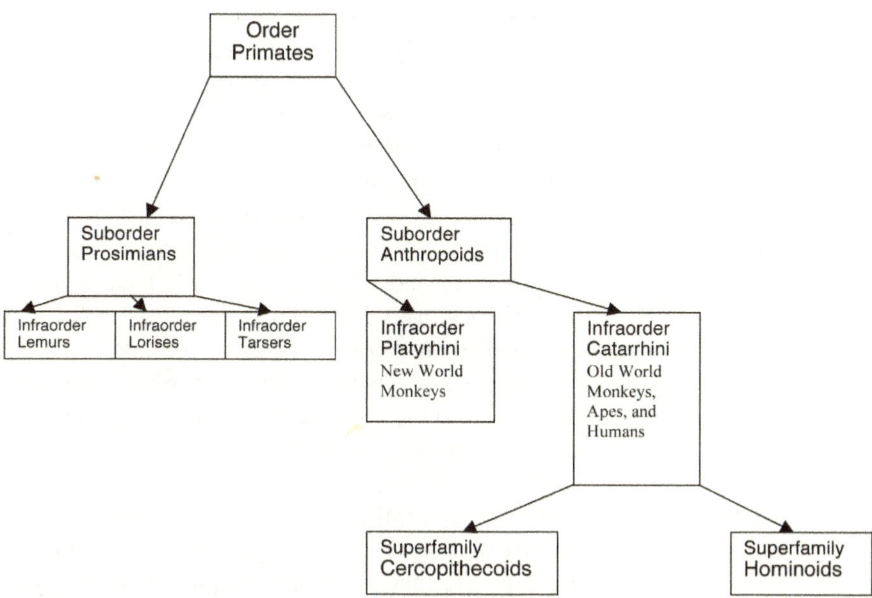

Figure 7.2. Primate Order Expanded. This depiction was created by the author.

Oligocene epoch or the end of the Eocene after anthropoids first supposedly originate.

Elwyn Simons, for example, an Oxford trained paleoanthropologist first working at Yale and now a Director at Duke University, has found fossils of early-formed anthropoids' front teeth dating back to 37 million years ago. The fossil of what is now called a *Catopithecus*, which has been considered the oldest higher primate or anthropoid, was found in the Fayum Desert in Egypt.[5] Simons not only found some of the oldest of what are called pithecines there in Egypt from the Jebel el Qatrani Formation, but also he found 21 different primate species from various prehistoric periods.[6] The Jebel el Qatrani Formation in the Fayum Depression of Egypt is dated at older than 31 m.y.a. old.[7]

A key archaeological site that had produced a great quantity of finds would be the Fayum Depression, which is distanced about sixty kilometers from the great center of the Giza Pyramids in Cairo. I would like to state here that unlike the tradition of prior venerated anthropologists both European and American a biased ancestral leaning will not be made. I am reminded that the task at hand is to unveil the processual and perpetual Western white tendencies of negating blackness. It seems that as we look back in time and search for origins as some anthropologists of the 1960s had done, e.g., Simons in particular, there is a need to look at not only localities that would yield the best preserved finds as those discovered primarily in dry regions which once had been wet and tropical and rich in thriving primate life forms, but also there is a need to search within the Africanic center of the planet as the only key locality that has helped to perceptively unlock the mysteries that perceptively work at insightfully understanding our prehuman origins.

Moreover, it would be interesting to see how other presently dry regions have fared as other archaeologists work at producing a profundity of fossil finds that reveal other discoverable origins. As has been the case with certain pockets of other dry places like Australia where the desperate white hunt is on to find origins other than those maintained in the African continent. It seems that the Eocene and Oligocene and in general in other localities has not yielded as much in primate finds worldwide as those found in the African continent. Presently still, however, there is only one early primate find that has been found and that represents a great deal. It seems that what I will call the aegyptopithecines and the propliopithecines from the Fayum area resemble the apes in one of the earliest periods of time. It is where we have to say the *Anthropoidea* would begin as the "*Aegyptopithecus* is the best-known Oligocene anthropoid."[8] If we are to continue our statement that concerns paleoprimatological connectivity and working within the model of a black/white dichotomy then we have to add that an archaic primate (black) Egyptian was part of the line that helped to proceed along in humanity's descent.

The Suborder of anthropoids begins to thrive in the Oligocene epoch and we find that morphological progression is occurring when we review the fossil finds and as paleoprimatology endeavors to explain the later appearances of what are called hominoids. A Suborder and Infraorder and, etc. etc. etc. with the prefixes of *super* meaning "above," *infra* meaning "below," and *sub* meaning "under" all borrowed from Latin and all work at dividing up a branch of scientifically devised relations that are perceived to have existed throughout the *Primates* evolution (see Figures 7.3 and 7.4). The term *Hominoidea* refers to what are called hominoids and this label is quite different than what is meant by anthropoid. The term hominoid is used as a shortened version of the Superfamily of *Hominoidea*, which as time proceeds we find that the forms that come in the Miocene fossil record are not quite as yet developed as to what comes after the preliminary beginnings of what are commonly referred to as hominids.

The word *hominid* refers to a later and closer human form than when the Superfamily of hominoids appear. The term *hominids* is a shortened translation for *Hominidae*, which is a word that means "humanlike creature" it stems from the Latin *homin,* which comes from the Latin nominative singular noun *homo* meaning "human." Forms within the Family of hominids are closer to humans on the descent line than forms from the general Superfamily of hominoids (again, see Figures 7.3 and 7.4). The last form that should be considered are what are called hominines or what can be considered as the Subfamily or Genus ("kind") of hominines, which again makes use of the Latin root *homin* and adds the suffix *ine* and which also refers to the forms that are "human *only*." Humans and their closest ancestors are in sense restricted to the subdivision of the *Hominidae* or hominids and then there is the subsequent subdivision after hominids appear in time, which is considered the Genus or Subfamily of *Homininae* or hominines. Bear in mind that the aegyptopithecine finds existed within the Superfamily of hominoids and are really small primates that appear early in the *Primates* descent tree branch and can still be considered evolutionarily extremely distant. The Oligocene and early Miocene hominoid connectivity to hominines is still considered quite speculative and still under research and investigation.

According to Simons, the aegyptopithecine finds were much earlier than the more generalized dryopithecines or *Proconsul africanus,* which are hominoids as well. The dryopithcines are very important in the paradigm of human evolution because they are somewhat numerous throughout the Miocene and as of recent in the archaeological record can be found in places outside of Africa such as Hungry, Pakistan, and Greece.[9] Nevertheless, Simons believes that his aegyptopithecine finds resembled other East African finds, particularly those hominoids of the Oligocene and Miocene epochs. He also believes that there were definitely "interrelationships" between many hominoids of the periods and he even wanted to place his *aegyptopithecus*

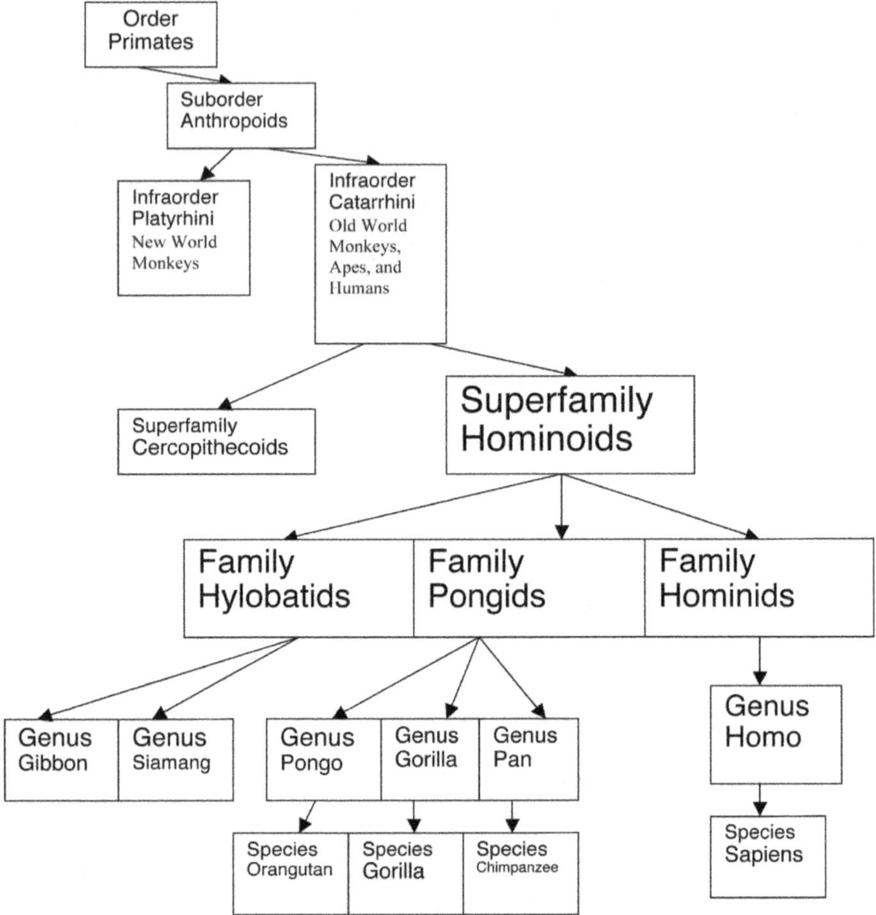

Figure 7.3. Primate Order Expanded Further. This depiction was created by the author.

specimen within the ancestry of *Proconsul.*[10] There is also enough evidence to believe that the Jebel el Qatrani Formation existed when the area had been a tropical rainforest environment and also that most of the primates found were living near large curving rivers that existed in the region at that time.[11] Simons continuously maintained "that many Egyptian Oligocene primates are likely to be in or near the ancestry of later monkeys, apes and men."[12] He contended against those Asian origin propounders (who I will refer to as propounders of "the old white *lux ex orientes* school-of-thought" of decades before) when he states that

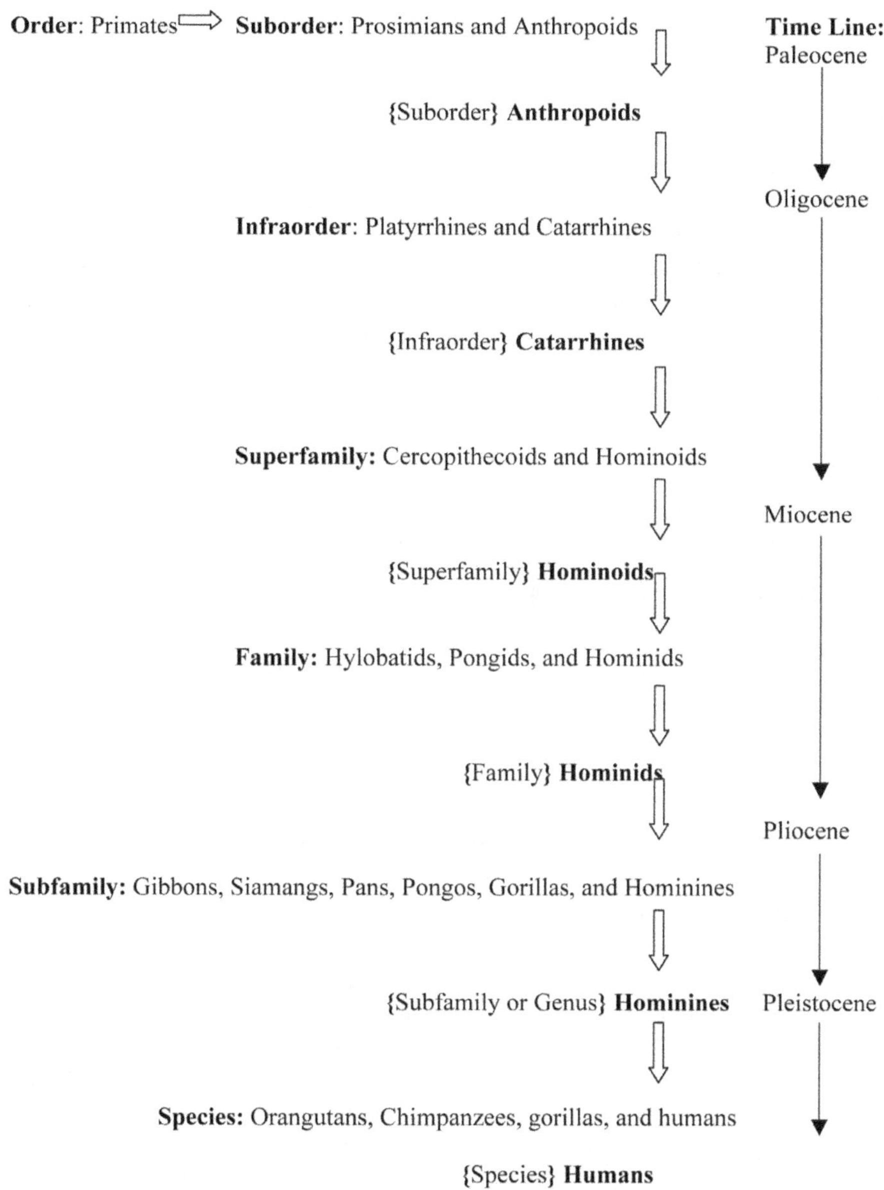

Figure 7.4. Primate Order and Timeline. This depiction was created by the author.

> [s]tudents of fossil mammals know that there is little evidence of the occurrence of higher primates (*Anthropoidea*) in the known Eocene, Oligocene and early Miocene fauna of Eurasia; thus pointing to the continent of Africa (where Oligocene and Miocene Primates are abundant) as the probable place of differentiation of monkeys, apes and men.[13]

Also, even back then, after the discovery of *Aegyptopithecus*, one of the closest forms we have to *Proconsul*, Simons urges that we need to discover more dryopithecines and we need more Oligocene-Miocene forms that transitioned for instance between *Propliopithecus haeckeli* and *Ramapithecus punjabicus.*[14] Propliopithecines by the way are one of the oldest forms that came before ramapithecines, and ramapithecines are the closest forms we have that come near the break between ape and preman. They are the root form to hominid appearance hence the Greek root term and title "*rama*."

Nevertheless, what becomes debatable is that these Fayum discoveries assert the earliest known anthropoids, which have been found predominantly in an Egyptian region or for that matter a North African site, a very faraway distance from the still believed originating and proto developing sites of Asia. Or for that matter they are very distant from the Miocene epoch Proconsuls that were the oldest of hominoids found in places like Rusinga Island in Kenya, i.e. in Kenya which is part of the great Kenyan, Tanzanian, and Ugandan trio that has brought us the oldest archaeological finds of hominids worldwide.

MIOCENE DISRUPTIONS

The Miocene epoch is part of a major division of the Tertiary period and it began around 24 m.y.a. and lasted until approximately 5 m.y.a. It is an important phase in primate evolution because at this time we begin to have increases in the number of larger primates that were known to exist throughout newly positioned Africa, Asia, and Europe after the breakup of the supercontinents Laurasia (Asia, Europe, and North America) and Gondwanaland (Africa, Antarctica, Australia, India, Madagascar, and South America). Again, as stated above in chapter 6 of this research, it seems that from 25 to 20 m.y.a. a large body of water called the Tethys Sea existed between the two supercontinents and it further divided the two land masses of Gondwanaland and Laurasia and also prevented the exchange of animals. It is also believed that hominoids after the break up were very limited. Previously before the geologic changes anthropoids were diversifying and colonizing Africa and Eurasia. Hominoids, on the other hand were somewhat united. It seems that geologic shifts have caused a great effect to our primatological prehistory.

According to a Berkeley scholar named Noel Boaz, back in the Miocene epoch and perhaps even as late as in the early Pliocene epoch the Sahara was a hospitable environment. And then unfortunately climatic changes occurred once again; massive Antarctic ice sheets and a colder and colder Antarctic region brought less and less evaporation over West and Central Africa. Boaz goes on to propose a hominid and chimp split with hominids moving east and chimps moving west. He goes on to say:

> We can be confident then in reconstructing the northern half of Africa in the late Miocene and early Pliocene as savanna and savanna woodland, but not desert. This is important because it demonstrates that the northern half of the continent was clearly a potentially habitable place for emergent hominids and has to be considered in hypotheses about hominid emergence. [15]

The North African region became a desert because of what has been referred to as Messinian initiated aridity in the Mediterranean Basin. Geologically it is proven that throughout the Oligocene and early Miocene this area was once vegetational. The Messinian event is a term used for describing the drying out of the Mediterranean Basin during 6 to 5 m.y.a. Boaz believed that the Missenian event, a very impacting climatic occurrence, had an effect on life and land. This affected hominid origin in a decisive manner. [16] Boaz's key hypothesis is that hominid origin begins in the (once tropical and forested) Sahara, not in the Eastern Rift Valley. [17] The presently archaeologically difficult condition for surveying the Sahara is to blame for severe scarcity of finds. Nonetheless given our current vacant fossil record, Boaz assures us that the Miocene site of Gebel Zelten in central Lybia will prove enhancing. [18]

Researchers also believe from various discoveries within the twentieth century that the origins of a variety of what are called early pithecines in particular the key linking dryopithecines and sivapithecines which have been found to date back to the Oligocene epoch, around 38–25 m.y.a., in Central Africa, Asia, and even Europe. The term pithecine or *pithecus* is a popular one and it comes from the Greek root word *pithekos* and it means "ape" or "monkey." The late date of the Messinian event in the Miocene epoch could explain not only the appearance of what are called austrolopithecines (or rather the forms considered *Australopithecus* which comes from the Greek use of *australo* and *pithekos* which literally translates to "southern apes" for they were initially thought to stem from the South African region), but also the disjunction of perhaps their existence in all the same multiple geographic regions of the early pithecines in particular of the australopithecines the successors to the dryopithecines and siviptithecines and the precursors to humanity.

It is traditionally believed that African apes and hominids arose from dryopithecines and it is supposed that the right kind of specific evolutionary forces existed to transform these intermediate level austrolopithecines (ape-like beings) to further changes into hominines.[19] And so, even with these discoveries in Egypt of early pithecines in the Miocene epoch one may consider how it was that later austrolopithecines (hominids) and the foraging and scavenging *Homo habilis* (a hominine) are found restricted from entering other regions than the East African corridor such as North Africa, Asia, and even Europe.

The ever slowly transforming primates of the Miocene epoch have been particularly commonly referred to as hominoids. Hominoids begin to date from the geologically turbulent Miocene times, but let us also note that the majority of hominoid fossils found from this particular epoch are mostly just teeth and jaws. Most of these teeth and jaws have been given several differing scientific names and what has increased in the descriptive science of hominoids is a hodge-podge of mostly quite inundating taxonomic labels. The confusion arises from attempting to classify the remains both as apes and non-apes, that is to say ape-like or monkey-like.[20] Some specimens are even closely reconstructed to relate to hominids.[21]

Now here it is important to note that when I refer to hominoids in this research I do not refer entirely to the superfamily of what are hominoids which encompass a great deal such as the (1) hylobatids (the lesser apes): gibbons and siamangs, (2) the pongids: sivapithecines, ramapithecines, orangutans, gorillas, bonobos, and chimpanzees and (3) the hominids: humans and their closest ancestors, and various australopithecines (see Figures 7.3 and 7.4). Rather and instead this research will solely concern itself with what has been referred to as humanity's nearest relative referred specifically as presented by paleoprimatologists not just as simply early forms but specific and generalized fossils that are commonly used to help explain the descent to humanity. Again, I am merely concerned with specific precursors to australopithecines that are believed to have been in existence since the Oligocene to the Miocene epochs. Early forms of these specific periods are believed to be theoretically prominent precursors in humankind's formulation.

There are endless categories that work at presenting a complexity of a perpetually re-devised past and science has stressed certain specific forms with minute detail of morphological teeth distinctions as the primary attestation of physical change. The early light-weight forms are believed to be one of humanity's earliest ancestors, which fall under the hominoid umbrella. Many hominoids are also commonly suffixed as pithecines and this title has been used for a great deal of finds that went on to distinguish all the varying types that exist within the hominoid subcategory of the family that makes up the hominids. Again, let us explicate and state that the *hylobatids* which comes from the Greek word *hylobates* and literally translates to mean "one that inhabits the woods," as the word is a combination of the Greek noun *hyle* "wood" with the Greek verb *bainein* which means "to go" and thus hylobatids are thought to be just that "inhabitants of the woods" or rather "those that thrive on tree." Hylobatids are considered the lesser apes like gibbons and they begin to appear in the record since the Pleistocene epoch.

Then there are the pongids the word, which came from a confusion of congo which came from Chinese for black tea. The word Pongid then came from the misused word *mpongo* which meant "fatness" or "obesity" and of course its intended use to refer to orangutans where "*o ray oo tan*" which came from the Malaysian word that refers to "wild man" "or "savage" and which of course was inappropriately borrowed by European scientists to regard the apes. The orangutans belong to the ancestors of Asia's sole living great apes and also included under the pongid category are the crucial Middle Miocene fossil finds that are known as the sivapithecines and ramapithecines. Both "siva" and "rama" finds have been described as early forms. Of particular paleoprimatological intrigue are the "siva" and "rama" forms, which also appears in the record right up to before and after the break off between prehuman and ape around 7 m.y.a.

Within all the varying forms of hominids, which come late in the Miocene record, what we have are anatomical subtleties that make their sequenced linearity quite complex. The decipherment of the anthropoid to hominoid to hominid to hominine fossil record is essential in order to ascertain the mechanics of evolutionary progress to humanity. The scientific classification process helps to give an appearance of uniformity and a forward moving liaison, which has been installed. Again, this enquiry will primarily certain itself with generally grouped early forms for the sake of pointing out a function of an installed scientific paradigm that explains the evolutionary and gradual appearance of humans and that traditionally helped to prop up a *racializing* construct.

Nevertheless, bear in mind that early forms were found not just in the southeastern African regions where most of our later evolutionary connected and well-publicized "nearman" hominids have been found, but also way up north in a region that had not been easily detected by nineteenth century intellectuals. Our enlightened scholars of the nineteenth century and our traditionalized historic past has helped to formulate, generally speaking as whole, the human origins and hypothesizing sciences which iterated new images of a metamorphic past that has now been abrogated by a supplanted and subsequently technologically induced scholar in a still yet quite cyclic and innovative *haut monde* that always seems to find better creative ways of inevitably recreating the Africanic.

NOTES

1. See Wyss and Flynn, p. 187–188, where phylogenetic taxonomy which is a system used to define what are called taxa or singular form taxon or just labels to clades or trees that present connections of life forms and according to Wyss and Flynn the label or name Anthropoidea is a

means to refer to "entities" of interest. See also Williams and Kay p. 189–190 where they argue that the Taxon *Anthropoidea* refers to a "descent community" but that there is a problem when we make use of providing "monotypic families" because of the distinctions made that causes exceptions and exclusions of characteristic and uncharacteristic forms which can be either stem- or crown-based and thus there should be no breaks or static restrictions (preDarwinistically) when it comes to grouping related forms.

2. P. 17.

3. On *Oligopithecus* and catarrhines where *Oligopithecus* is considered a nonanthropoid please see Rosenberger p. 75 for discussion on problems of perceptions on anthropoidal form transitions.

4. See *Cambridge Encyclopedia of Human Evolution* (1988 edition), p. 199.

5. Haviland p. 123 who cites Culatta, E. p. 1851

6. Simons had been searching in this area for quite some time for early claims on fossil apes see Simons (1963) and (1965).

7. Simons (1967) and Fleagle (1986) p. 131.

8. See *Cambridge Encylclopedia* p. 207.

9. See Benefit and McCrossin p. 240.

10. (1987 [1978]) p. 146.

11. Fleagle (1986) p. 131.

12. (1987[1978]) p. 147.

13. (1987[1978]) p. 147.

14. (1987[1978]) p. 150.

15. P. 99.

16. Ibid. p. 92.

17. Ibid. p. 104. Also, Potts p. 76–77 asserts climatic alterations in particular in Africa between 6.4–4.6 m.y.a. which coincides with the Messinian Crisis and this ecological event appears simultaneously with a primary African hominid development.

18. Boaz uses Simons (1984) find to support a paleoecological assertion (his label: hypothesis #3) that northern Africa was forested during the Miocene epoch, p. 105.

19. Haviland p.134.

20. According to Rose p. 193 Miocene hominoids are neither ape-like nor monkey-like and he cautions that we should "refrain from absolute similarities" because they were "Miocene hominoid-like."

21. Stein and Rowe p. 244.

Chapter Eight

Ape-like to Human-like Taxonomy *Ad infinitum*

EARLY AFRICANIC TRANSFORMATIVES

In general, extinct early forms of primates were found in North Africa and some could presume a great deal about the paleodemography. Certainly, if early forms are found high up in the North African regions one could reason and further infer that there should have been a logical propensity for a continual dispersal of our ever-so-consistently transforming early forms into proximities outside of a separating Africa so as to remain in places like Europe and north western Asia even after the breakup of Laurasia. They could have continuously prolonged in accordance with the same evolutionary developments as we find within Africa. They could have adapted to colder environments and they could have changed in form other than what we have found in Africa as what has been commonly believed to occur with the later forms of *Homo erectus* and *Homo sapiens*. Early forms could have upheld similitude in combination with corrective evolutionary adaptive forces as seen profusely displayed in the fossil record.

Another lucid assumption concerning the origination and dispersal of early forms of hominoids is that they did exist in North Africa as surely as they did maintain the opportunity to venture and persist in a late Miocene Eurasia. There had always been a surviving ecological need to travel further east and out of Africa as the fossil record displays later on in our prehistory with in particular the later forms of *Homo erectus* and archaic *sapiens*. Multiple forces were always challenging the early forms and they proved that they could persist for a time. From the archaeological record we can note that extinct early forms were found in various places outside of Africa such as Europe and North America.

Despite the fact that we find extinct early forms of primates particularly those of the Miocene epoch in various places outside of Africa, as of yet, as time went on and new forms appeared in the archaeological record, in regards to the distinct later forms of australopithecines, we have not found any fossils outside of African soil, and as far as concerns these later forms of pithecines during the Pliocene epoch (again particularly prominent australopithecine types) we have never found not one specimen in any remotely distant location. All that we do have are just interpretations on "crude tools" that have been reported outside of Africa. [1]

It must be remarked here that this analysis specifically regards the extinct Miocene hominoids because they have been theoretically assembled by physical anthropologists in order to help explain the life-forming process that led to the origins of prehumanity or for that matter humanity. The particularly prominent critical groups: the governing label of the *Proconsul* which is based in Africa, the *Ramapithecus* and *Sivapithecus* from the Asian region and the expansive *Dryopithecus* group both African and European forms were once thought of as quite useful in understanding the evolutionary process that displays the predevelopments of humanity. Let me first begin generally with these extinct early forms of hominoids. Hominoids like the dryopithecines and the sivapithecines ranged remarkably enough widely throughout nonAfrican regions, such as Asia, and Europe. [2] Many scientists no longer question whether these particular pithecines, also once considered the prototypical pre-eminence of hominids, existed in prehistoric times and some scholars no longer doubt that from a select portion of these varied pithecines there developed evolutionary avenues of transformance that persisted and stem on up to hominids and of course humans, which again must obviously incorporate the consideration of long durational and time-based multi-millennial adaptative processes. [3]

Since the prominent *Proconsul* hominoids were first discovered in East Africa in 1926 at Koru, Kenya it was assumed that evolutionary developments would also be proven to have continued throughout in the nonAfrican regions with the nonAfrican versions of early forms, and yet this had not been the case. In regards to the *Proconsul Africanus* there are several Miocene Kenyan primary sites with rich finds of early hominoids, such as in the Songhor and Rusinga Islands, where in the Rusinga Island for example we even find KNM-RU 2036CH, a scapula, proximal humerus. There is no other part of the world that can yield thousands of specimens as those found from mostly Africa and except for the *Proconsul* versions found only in Africa in the fossil record we have mostly discovered teeth and jaws. [4] Allow me to state that teeth and fragments of jaws are an archaeologically fossilized element that preserves quite well so it seems and of course especially well in the dry eastern portions of Africa. Unfortunately, however, most scientific assertions about Miocene pithecine evolutionary developments are derived from teeth predominately and yet the most important thing that we can assess from teeth is what were these pithecines eating and what changes occurred from changing diets that would also mean changing environments that are reflected from changing eating habits.

Please allow me to further once again point out that generally the early prominent hominoids that Western science considers as playing a critical role in the transitional development of prehumanity had all been assessed from these extinct pithecine fossil finds that can actually be viewed as being no bigger than gibbons. The first and foremost leader of these extinct early forms is what has been called *Proconsul*. It has been given the imperial Roman title of *Proconsul* because it had been considered just that the provincial governor or high-ranking official of provinces or colonies in place of the *consul*, and hence the use of the prefix *pro*. The early form is an early Miocene hominoid and one of the oldest of the early pithecines that holds the genus and pithecine title of *Proconsul,* which had been (again let me) add initially described in 1926 from fossils discovered at Koru, Kenya.

It is believed that *Proconsul*, an extinct primitive early form of the African Miocene that was related to the next form, that I will soon talk of, the dryopithcines, became quite diversified and permutated into several species (or "forms") in the early Miocene epoch of East Africa and it must be remembered that its fossil remains were first believed to have been the remains of the great ape or pongid[5] before it was given its own scientific category. Proconsul maintains very primitive features, which is why it is considered as still somewhat un-apelike especially if we notate its prominent facial prognathic features and lack of bulging brow ridges; however, *Proconsul Africanus*' lack of a tail has helped to add it to an apelike connection or trajectory at least. Unfortunately, the *Proconsul's* directed end line of evolutionary destination has not been met; scholars still remain quite speculative about its evolutionary morphological connectedness given that they have not found similarly and plausible close transitive forms.

Nonetheless, proconsuls are considered somewhat related to dryopithecines. The next crucial extinct early form that has garnered a great deal of attention is what has been called dryopithecines. *Dryopithecus* presented here as a generalized homonoid that once thrived in Africa can also be found in Europe and the name *Dryopithecus* is a term that makes use of the Greek word *dryo*, which comes from *dry(s)* and is the Greek word for "tree" or "oak." Thus, the dryopithecines were considered apes or monkeys from the trees. And so, just as the classical mythic dryads or nymphs of the woods, they were considered rustic inhabitants of what were the nearby European forests with their oak trees. They differed from those of living apes in that their incisors were smaller.

When we turn to dryopithecines we find that scholars primarily still do hold to the idea that early hominids have originated from a Miocene ape, perhaps a dryopithecine-like form. Dryopithecines date to around 13–11 m.y.a. (in what could be called the Middle Miocene epoch) and they have generally been grouped under one genus, they also are known to have also scattered into or been indigenous to various places outside of Africa, that is to places in France, Spain, Italy, Greece, Austria, and Hungary.[6] The Greek and Hungarian versions are somewhat similar, but have been maintained separately. Most of the Miocene hominoids have been found to be somewhat geographically diverse. A family of dryopithecines spread over a wide area in the Old World and it was once believed that these were the "progenitors" that led to the lines that gave us the present races of humans.[7] Since dryopitheicnes are discovered far off from Africa it was once commonly believed that these were the precursors that led to variegated and unfortunately "*racialized*" humanity. There were direct primatological descendancy outside of Africa and links have been asserted to be multipliable and diversely located.

There is no doubt that the evolutionary patterns that delve that far back are somewhat complex and the scientific descriptive explanations that scholars have come to use have varied from "apelike" to "humanlike."[8] We are still making taxonomic revisions on these Miocene hominoidal forms.[9] We would again have to question parallel evolutionistic theorems that maintain newly re-devised paradigms and which produce strict identifying guidance. Again, there can be no doubt that established proponents of the Modern Synthesis have helped to solidify an anatomical and asserted continuum between prior-ape and prior-human to present-human. There is still an intense need to find the common ancestor of the Miocene epoch.

When we study the dryopithecines we find what has been commonly referred to as the Y-5 arrangement where a regularity of molar cusps and fissure patterns have helped to standardize this group. Samples have been found from Hungary (*Rudapithecus*), Spain (*Dryopithecus laietanus*), and China *(Dryopithecus Keiyanensis*). Remember that we had by the end of 20 m.y.a. an end to the separation of the supercontinents Gondwanaland and Laurasia, and yet it is believed that by the Middle Miocene times the African tectonic plate came into contact with the Euro-Asiatic plate and a land connection was well on its way to being formed. The fossil record displays a reciprocal migrational process where Asiatic species came into Africa and African species (along with hominoids came into Asia). The land bridges formed from about 16–14 m.y.a.[10]

Again as stated in previous chapters of this analysis tectonic plate movement due to inevitable geologic shifting have always contributed to a changing climatic world where pieces of land and even continents have relocated. As would happen with tectonic plate movement as a piece of Africa collides with Asia, the end result was development of mountainous regions along with climatic changes, which of course would have affected the fauna and flora. From these geo-maneuvering activities came a decrease in tropical forests and hence due to a lessening expansive precipitation caused by increased mountainous developments there came an increase in savanna grasslands.

It is believed that these Middle Miocene climatic changes caused the further radiation and transformation of the hominoidal process.[11] Even what has been called the European pliopithecines found after these Miocene geoactivities have been used to attest to hypothetical propulsive species diffusional forces at work. The dryopithecines that have been found in all the various regions out of Africa have been consolidated into a generalized form and yet it is believed that their precursors must have originated in Africa since the oldest finds as of yet come from there. The dryopithecine-generalized form seems to present morphous or rather dentinine alteration that presents these discovered forms as the closest evidence we have to that mysterious point between hominid and ape fissure for their canine teeth are larger than those of humans, but they are not as strongly developed as those of modern apes. This is predominantly the reasoning behind past held beliefs that dryopithecines gave rise to the modern gorilla and chimpanzee and also it is believed that an ancestral animal looking like a dryopithecine gave rise to a derivative form that eventually led to australopithecines and then to closer humanlike forms and subsequently to humans.

It was once the common belief that dryopithecines led the way to reaching to humanity (see Figure 8.1). Although the fossil record remains scant when it comes to these kinds of forms of hominids, legitimate cases of transitive forms are needed that can be identified as progressions towards humanity. Yet persistent descriptive analytical trends making use of branches or what are scientifically referred to as clades based on interpretable characteristics have helped to prove some structural advancement. One may wonder as to why the great God or force of Natural Selection has chosen these early forms of pithecines over all other species given that through the great expansive prehistoric time-span mammalian forms have had some brain increases, but as evidenced by studies on encephalizations none have had as grand a scale of growth as that for pithecines throughout their endless millenary transformitive existence.

Nevertheless, the next somewhat important extinct early forms from the Miocene epoch are what are called sivapithecines and ramapithecines, which were first found in the Siwalik Hills of Pakistan. Sivapithecines were once formerly known as ramapithecines as well and that is why today they continue to maintain close affiliation with what are commonly referred to as ramapithecines.[12] Sivapithecines were also found in the Candir sites and Pasalar in Turkey, Lu-feng in China. Also, the ones found in the Potwar Plateau, Pakistan held close facial resemblances to the orangutan and this essentially is why most scholars have made a radiated line for an ancestral connection to orangutans from sivapithecines. The prefix *Siva* actually comes from the

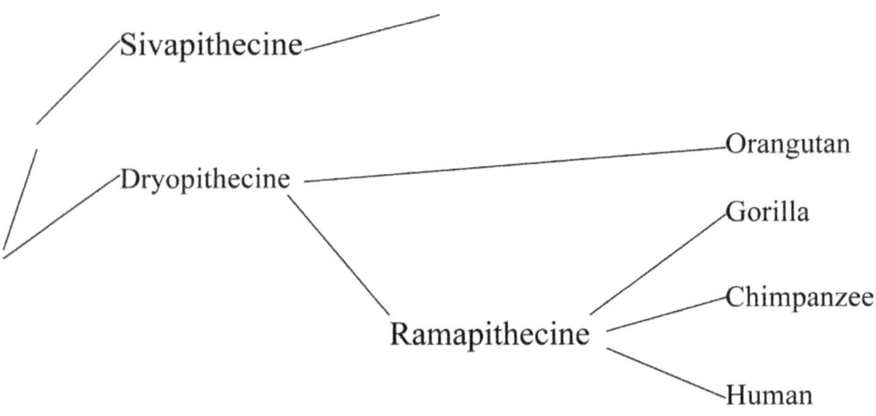

Figure 8.1. Pithecine Trajectory. This depiction was created by the author.

Sanskrit word *shiva*. *Shiva* is also the male Hindu name for the third member of a great triad, Shiva the Destroyer along with Brahma the Creator and Vishnu the Preserver made up a powerful Trinitarian-like force. The name *siva* also signifies in Sanskrit "of good omen." Shiva destroys and can be considered a potent force that bore skulls of various sorts as he resides on Mt Kailas, a northern peak of the Himalayas.

The ramapithecines were found in both India and Pakistan and formerly thought to be a possible human ancestor. The Sanskrit prefix term *rama* actually comes from the *Ramayana*, any of the three avatars of *Vishnu*, (1) *Balarama*, (2) *Parashurama* or (3) *Ramachandra*. *Rama* is the hero of the Indian epic poem Ramayana. An incarnation of the god Vishnu, Rama is one of the chief objects of Hindu worship of a supreme being in human form. The *Ramayana* is the shorter of the two great Sanskrit epics of India the other being the author's favorite titled Mahabharata which has some Illiadic similar themes. Our fossil finds of *Ramapithecus* are known from teeth and jaw fragments. Both the sivapithecines and ramapithecines are predominantly Asian extinct forms and the former is believed to be the ancestor of orangutans and the latter of baboons. Nevertheless, in Africa itself there is the *Kenyapithecus* form that is found in East Africa and that has been considered a primitive form of a ramapithecine. There is little difference between the *rama* and *dryo* forms and *Kenyapithecus* comes very close, but until we find limb bones we will not know for sure how close the forms were to hominids and in this case humanity.

A particular evidentiary ramapithecine is *Ramapithecus punjabicis,* which was discovered in 1934 by an American paleontologist named G. E. Lewis. It was found in the Siwalik Hill Miocene deposits in northwest India where sivapithecines have been generally found. Lewis himself believed the *Ramapithecus punjabicis* find to be a hominid, or rather a descendant of humans, but of course this was not well received given the then well-established creationistic antagonisms. Simons and Pilbeam have long since resurrected Lewis's specimen and have confirmed its hominid characteristics.[13] Leakey's *Kenyapithecus wickeri* has been also considered yet another form of a ramapithecine. What makes the ramapithecines so critical is that they represent advancement over the sivapithecines even if the latter come toward a teleological end. It was customarily believed that *Ramapithecus punjabicus* was the earliest known hominid in the fossil record, dating to perhaps 14–12 m.y.a. of course this was the belief until things in paleontology began to change by the 1980s with further new archaeological finds.

Contentions about just when the hominids begin are long standing. Attempting to piece together the morphological progression of primates remains a daunting task. In the black/white dichotomous spectrum by the twenty-first century we should not find doubt that an African origin would remain victorious in having the oldest finds. Long ago attempts had been made to look towards the eastern horizons as where the sun rises and as where also humanity. In the early twentieth century we found that science had been still plagued by the interminable quest to turn to the East and to find our early forms in Asia.[14] There can be little doubt that science (anthropologists in particular) has always been hard at work at finding not only Asian finds but also even European finds that worked at proving European ancestral links to the time of the early anthropoids.[15] There are toils and toils of troubles as science continued to find better and more useful white constructs.

RAMADUS: THE OLDEST REMNANT

Lastly, I turn to the extinct early form referred to as A*rdipithecus* and which is one of the later dated pithecines. Ardipithecines date to as late as 4.4 m.y.a., in the archaeological record and they are found at Aramis in the Middle Awash region of Ethiopia.[16] This is a new genus that also is believed to have established the way for the beginnings of the standard australopithecines.[17] Some scholars would even go as far as to state that *Ardiipithecus ramidus*[18] is a species that lies close to the point in hominoid evolution where near-human hominids first begin to split off from modern apes.[19] Many persuasive interpreters on origins would maintain from ardipithecines that an Ethiopian human origin theory could be validated.[20] The ardipithecine is considered a hominid because the foramen magnum is more forward than in apes and because of the teeth and of the elbow joint. It is very close to the consensus date of the hominid-ape split.[21]

Nevertheless, *Ardipithecus* is a closely linked form to the sivapithecine and rampithecine stock. And although it appears toward the end of the turbulent Miocene epoch or perhaps to others it appears in the earliest part of the Pliocene, it remains a debatable form and has been identified as one of the first ancestral hominids. The insurmountable fact that it only appears in Africa adds further significance to the African centric base that had immensely helped in the predevelopment stages of extinct early forms that assisted in maintaining our present human teleological destination. What do we make of the various non-African extinct early finds? We learn to better understand the connectivities and learn not to allow for overly enthusiastic stress on the dissimilarities of African and non-African early forms and accept the similarities as a revealing sign that we are all truthfully derived from one base.

NOTES

1. Brace p. 48 has suppositioned only that variants of what he calls "pithecanthropine sites" have been found outside of Africa.
2. Haviland, p. 127 and also see Boaz p. 45, who argues that apes traveled out of Africa back in the Miocene when places like Europe and Asia were densely tree populated, even elephants had found their way to Asia and along with them came apes. See also Brace p.103. See Conroy p. 85 who asserts that Miocene hominoids appear in Western Europe (France) in about 16 m.y.a.
3. Haviland, p. 134 and Brace, p. 140.
4. Conroy, p. 94–95.
5. Conroy, p. 97.
6. Whittaker, p. 233. Turnbaugh et al. [see biblio.].
7. Wolpoff (1997), p. 143 talks of Earnest A. Hooton's [p. 572–573] evolutionary theory propounded in the early part of the twentieth century. Also at one time polygenism saw races as separate human species. Also see Wolpoff (1997) p. 145 for assetion that Hooton believed different races came from differing dryopithecines.
8. Whittaker, p. 232.
9. Conroy, p. 116.
10. Stein and Rowe p. 246–247.
11. Ibid. p. 246.
12. Conroy p. 110 states that back in the 60's and 70's there was a predominant idea held that both the sivapithecines and ramapithecines were in the direct human evolutionary lineage. The Chinese still maintain this belief. *ibid.* But for the most part Conroy p. 111 asserts orangutan-like similarities. He sees p. 112 sivapithecines and ramapithecines as being morphologically descriptive of sexual dimorphism, each being perspective representatives of either male or female forms.
13. See Simons and Pilbeam's famous article particularly pp. 114-117 where they argued that the dryopithecines should even have a tripartite subdivision that would include dryopithecines, proconsul and sivapithecine and thus where the ramapithecines would be grouped instead with the later forms of hominids p. 116.
14. See Ciochon (1985) where (Eocene epoch finds) in central Burma help to present a construct for an Asian birthplace for anthropoids.
15. See Zapfe p. 428–29 where back in the 1960s it was hoped that a new discovery of an early anthropoid in central Europe would not end the exhausted long quest to prove (or better yet create) a European anthropoidal origin construct.

16. Haviland. p.138. Conroy p. 84 refers to this form using the new label of australopithecus ramadus. Also he states that this form lived in African woodlands, as specimens of fauna and flora are typical of woodland have been found together with these hominids.

17. See White *et al.* (1994) for introduction of the new form.

18. In the Afar language *ardi* means "ground" or "floor" and *ramid* is the word for "root" and as the name implies.

19. Stein and Rowe p. 257. Potts p. 79 states that *ramadus* is the oldest we have from the split. On the other hand Megarry p. 136 states that it is the most ape-like and primitive hominid and yes closest to the divergence, but its status is still ambiguous.

20. Barrett on p.74 asserts that within Black Rastaferrian tradition the word "Ethiopia" takes on Biblical meaning and the word designates all of Africa including Egypt. Ethiopia becomes symbolic of all "burnt faces" as in Greek ancient times and not just a specified geographic region but it is the place believed to be the origin of all humanity.

21. Feder (3rd ed.) p. 196 who also cites White et al. (1994).

Chapter Nine

The Perpetuity of Divisiveness

STREAMLINED ADAPTION

George Lauder, a comparative methodologist on adaption has asserted in a prolific scientific work that, "in general there is widespread recognition of the fact that natural selection acts to alter biological organization based on currently available variation and not with anticipation of an endpoint in the future."[1] Changes that have occurred throughout time do not anticipate environmental challenges; on the contrary, some scientists have seen them as chance based responses. Whatever works at the moment keeps on working and whatever does not work is eliminated. We have modifications as a responding activity to a particular ecological situation and sometimes modifications help increase the population. These randomly occurring changes help the group persist, and sometimes the responses do not occur at all and the group becomes extinct.

Adaptations of archaic hominoids such as the early forms cannot be futuristically based; they can be considered reactive responses. The problem becomes where to place the discoveries of these proposed prehistoric prehominid links, these plausible progenitorial pithecine-like forms that have been located at various sites throughout the world. How do they fit within the macrocosmic contours of our aimless and yet seemingly precursored drive to what I call prehumanity? The present complexities of deciphering hominoidal propensity from an archaeologically and an interminably rediscoverable fossil record cannot be resolved even as further anthropological and biogenetical suppositions work hard at better explaining our trajectory from prehuman existence to the here and now in the twenty-first century.

In considering the long traveled evolutionary course diagramed by paleontologists, and naturalists and populational biologists alike, various scientists have speculated on humanoidal changes that are created to seem streamlined in fashion and well ordered. In a very scientific presentation let us turn to a molecular geneticist who elaborates on adaptational tendencies. According to Wade,

> Most adaptions are not determined by single loci, but rather require the coordinated action of many genes to produce behavioral, morphological, or physiological phenotypes. Gene interaction or epistasis in biochemical genetics occurs when the "expression of one gene wipes out the phenotypic expression of another gene" (Lewin 1990, p. 809). In evolutionary genetics, the *epistasis* variance (along with the dominance variance) is a populational quantity that measures the statistical effects of variations among individuals in gene combinations in relation to the total phenotypic variance. When multiple loci are involved in the determination of a trait, new features of selection within and among groups arise that are not captured by the single locus models. These new features can enhance the evolutionary role of population subdivision and interdemic selection and diminish the role of selection within groups... When demes are genetically isolated from one another a favorable gene combination may achieve high frequency within a local deme by a combination of random genetic drift and adaptive selection.[2]

Wade's statement on adaption leads this enquiry to regard the outside (non-African) hominoid to hominid desistencies. Outsiders (i.e. nonAfrican hominoids) did not maintain continuity as prehumanity evolves further. Various extinct hominoids did not progress and/or carry similar or even variant phenotypic form in a higher existential level or rather maintained in a progressed form as that held by the solely and subsequently advanced African hominids.

Standard formulaic evolutionary changes and a regional continuity did persist as it did with the African hominids. It seems that "random genetic drift" (an essential factor indeed) for variance had contributed to varying forms of early pithecines, but to a certain extent we can conclude that the African based hominids, in particular, the early hominids of the Late Miocene and Early Pliocene, remained in one geographic area namely East Africa. There is the belief, however, that repeated variance occurs with early humans at multiple pocketed sites as defended primarily by those I call "the all-African negating multiregionalists." Some scholars commonly believe that anatomical changes occur in a punctualistic fashion within long periods of stasis.

According to the multiregionalists it is because of nonAfrican based diffusional existences that were precipitated by various strategically environmental sites, such as newly evolved out-of-African savannas and forested areas that later human and so-called "races" have evolved from, and so it has been concluded that the originating appearance of early post-divided and simian-derived humans is not only multidimensional in distinguishing physical qualities but also always has had polygeographical promptings that inextricably were connected diachronologically both to later pithecines and to archaic early humans.

Again, the next rational question in our investigation is if there were connecting lines how was it that the nonAfrican lines come to die off as they inevitably did? As of yet, for example, the fossil record has not produced nonAfrican australopithecines. Why were nonAfrican links dating back from the Miocene and entering even the Pliocene become somewhat visibly terminus? Links are not what we need to look for since some have argued that evolutionary change does occur in "breaks" (as again through an exceptionally long stasis and a punctuated equilibrium).[3] Others have added that under an allopartic speciation process (i.e. another parted or rather divided species) model change can invariably be led to occur somewhere else in small peripheral and isolated regions away from an originating parent.[4] When we consider the fossil record we do note that group separation is an important element as well as climatic variation. Group separation may account for phenotypic (physical) and even genotypic (genetic) diversity and biologists have completed studies tracing these varying typic exposures that as of yet may not clearly be archaeologically visible. And thus, it can be explained that archaeological invisibility can be due to what has been considered evolutionary breaks. When we discover appearances and disappearances one can argue that what we have are "breaks" as natural selection continues its lumpy outstretched course. It is the concept of minutiae of breaks that seem to cause all the trouble in scientific reconstructions of humanity's evolutionary past. The breaks are what cause us to see discontinuity in a microcosmic sense.

One can also argue that the scarcity of later Miocene, for example, or rather early Pliocene nonAfrican hominids is not part of a disjunction, but instead it is a component of long conjunctive and cohesive breaks that may have been pivoted by geographical and ecological and isolationistic factors. Here "breaks" in the fossil record can be seen when we lack intermediate forms between long drawn-out and geographically specified species progressivity as we currently have within the record. Also, we must bear in mind that the question of stasis and punctuationism is one that still to this day remains debatable. There are micro-level disconnectivities amidst all the Miocene hominoidal pithecines that separate and divide, this would explain the need for multiple labels for the endless varieties that have been manifested in the scientific world where of course white conducive titles and white palatable labels help to make comprehensible the otherwise motley syndrome that can be our past. According to John Maynard Smith who is an eminent British evolutionary biologist, and an author of many books on evolution, both for scientists and the general public, what may be needed in order to bring an end to all the labeling and disjunction will be an end-all statistical analysis of the entire fossil record.[5] And thus, as of yet we have only come to nearly a fraction of the amount.

As it now stands we solely maintain inferences on separatistic entities without coherent recognizable sequentialism. Streams of replacement can be explained by an exceptionally slow phyletic gradualism which otherwise would be seen as disconnected pockets of pithecine existences. Perhaps one could argue as nineteenth century polygenicists once did that independent developments occurred with low frequency levels of finds in nonAfrican areas, the numbers of nonAfrican pithecine descendants, given the then set environmental constrictors, became just too low, thus this would explain the archaeological record's invisibilities. African pithecine transitional forms may have occurred in "pop up" fashion as they are found and thus can be considered to have appeared in a pocketed and concentrative environmentally habitable locality.

Lastly, on this matter of transitional invisibilities, we may come to consider again the famous Oxford trained zoologist Richard Dawkins who further argues that evolutionary change through, for example, a punctuated equilibrial form does occur between long periods of stasis that would seem rightly invisible to microevolutionists. He further points out that

> what a palaeontalogist sees as a saltation can in fact be a smooth and gradual change so slow as to be undetectable to the microevolutionist. This kind of palaeontological "saltation" has nothing to do with the one-generation macromutations that, I suspect Huxley and Darwin had in mind when they debated *Natura non facit saltum*.[6]

The point that Dawkins and other defenders of Darwinian gradualism are making is that we have not discovered all the pieces of the puzzle that will enable us to make a clear picture of what really happens in the past as Whole Life generally progresses. We are always in doubt about how reflective the record can be as it now stands. There are factors that sometimes can remain unconsidered, such as the belief that what we have and where we find fossils needed to have been biogeographically or environmentally dry enough and just right and perservable enough in order to contain the remnants of organisms as we find them and to exhibit for us the mannerisms of Whole Life as it passes through time. We must remember that not all locations are precisely dry enough to maintain bones as far back as we have found them in certain specified regions. The notion of invisibilities is tangential and therefore we may forever reside in the land of *Theoretica.*

Along with invisibilities we must remind ourselves that great scientific thinkers still struggle over and repeatedly ponder about the present identity of this self-corrective macromutating force that encodes at various microcosmic genetic loci and that can be read in a well-ordered scientific and destined fashion as unrecognizable manifestations that accrue each punctualistic moment after punctualistic moment.

Furthermore, it must be noted that this regulatory force in a mystifiable way has allowed Miocene hominoids to change into Pliocene early hominids and then into Pleistocene better-equipped hominids and then into Pleistocene archaic human. Moreover, this munificent force that science has a difficult time simplifying allowed for such a case as a group of apes living on a boundary of drying forests and widening savannas to begin yet another manner of questing for survival on the newly formed ground. Can the fossil record ever help us envision a snapshot portrait of this mystical kind of burst of change? Will further and further scions of devised and re-devised scientific explanations of evolution continue to elude the present contemplative human?

BEAST–PREHUMAN DEMARCATION

It is the boundaries between human beings and animals that become more symbolic for anthropologists because they tend to need to maintain a kind of "human uniqueness" in order to better continue their discourse on prehuman paleo-developments. We must remember that our purposeful existence depends on the demarcation or rather better yet as Cartmill, the Chicago-trained Duke Professor of the strong-house Biological Anthropology and Anatomy department, states, "the line that our culture draws between people and beasts is a moral as well as a conceptual boundary." Cartmill continues to add that

> because the animal-human boundary is the boundary of the moral universe, the stories that we tell about human origins even if they are true stories, are myths; and the general point of those stories is explaining—and legitimating—human control and domination of nature.[7]

One can also further add to Cartmill's indictment that the sciences (as a self-validating *explanator* of origins) continue to "anthropologize" (my term) about humanity's past worlds and continue to present existences that include the separation and development from apes via the endless evolutionary defended models and paradigms. When we refer to paradigms and models we regard the use of endless multi-variegated formats: orthogenesis, polygenesis, multiregionalism, punctualism, gradualism, punctualistic gradualism, natural selectionistic patterns, cladisms, fissurisms, etc., etc., etc. Notate that we will always maintain propriety on remade selves. Or better yet, we will always find a little beast in each and every one of us that perhaps still bears some qualities carried onwards from a Miocene beast abstraction. We have recreated newly formulated conceptions as we perennially delve into our past and find more and more remains. And as we continue to find varying forms and differing resemblances it is natural selection that seems to forever mystify.

It is believed that humans are connected to the Primates Order because we extensively share some basic characteristics in our anatomy, physiology, molecular structure and genetic material. A split between apes and prehumans has been claimed as occurring six million years ago.[8] It is quite unlikely that a three way split (human, chimpanzee, and gorilla) occurred at the same evolutionary moment, but instead some scholars believe that we first had a one lineage split followed by a subsequent human and chimpanzee split later on.[9] The noted science journalist Roger Lewin presents this split and depends on the work of Charles Sibley an ornithologist and a former Director at Yale Peabody Museum of Natural History and Jon Ahlquist, two pathbreaking researchers who worked on DNA-DNA hybridization comparisons between humans and great apes. DNA-DNA hybridization comparisons involve recombinations of different species DNA strands. These recombined DNA strands are reheated and then scientists time how long it takes for the strands to separate, the longer it takes to separate the closer the link.

Back in 1984 the Yale team concluded that by 8 to 10 m.y.a. there had been a first split then afterward by 6.3 to 7.7 m.y.a there came a second split which included human and chimpanzee.[10] Well over three million years ago in the Pliocene epoch we find that close fossil relations between apes and transitory hominids have been maintained. It is also believed that hominid life existed two million years ago or more. From a span of time of nearly two million years ago to just over 10,000 years ago (within the Pleistocene) it seems that most of our final evolutionary hominine development occurs. Science tells us that we are inextricably tied to a beast a beast that now remains visible not only in the microscopic world of laboratories, but also that remains in a macrocosmic sense in the black crevice of our minds. Humanity is recent both in the fossil record and in the molecular record, proposed links have been constructed at both levels the fossil record is used to buttress the molecular record and the latter is used to validate imagined objects that we cannot see with our natural eyes. Scientific constructs are forever at work attempting to create a clearer and whiter vision of the darkened past a past that still remains deeply hidden in the crevice of our abysmal minds.

The concept of demarcation performs within a white construct that forever toils at inching forward even within the specter of a better united and benevolent twenty-first century and where we find still improvisations on entity divides that have been led by making note of, for example, such genetic markers as HERV-K in the case of junk field transposons and FOXP2 in the case of the title for the gene that identifies language.[11] In a metamorphic sense the concept of demarcation enabled by white constructs have always helped to maintain the use and abuse of divisive polarities, the beast and the human, the them and the us, the rich and the poor, the European and the African, the Anglo-American and the African-American, the oppressor and the oppressed, the American and the anti-American, the Caucasian and the African, the Christian and the Islamic, the Semite and the anti-Semite, the outsider and the insider, etc., etc., etc.

NOTES

1. P. 63.
2. P. 397.
3. Gould and Eldridge, Gould and Lewontin, Gould and Vrba, and Eldridge (1985). Also against all of these articles and school of thought see Richard Dawkins (1996) p. 211 who sees punctuated equilibrium as not true saltationism, i.e. not macromutational.
4. Tattersall (1995) p. 162.
5. Pp. 198–99, J.M. Smith presents the viewpoint that Darwin was a gradualist and that gradual change is a manesfestation of the natural whereas on the other hand the sudden can be construed as a form of the supernatural. Also J.M. Smith presents himself as tending more toward gradualistic change. There are no spirits of "hopeful monsters." There is a need to analyze the "*bauplans*" (major patterns) of organization that are observable in the natural world. *Bauplan* is a German word that could also mean, "blueprint" or even technically also mean "fundamental body plan."
6. Dawkins (1996) p. 211.
7. (1990) p. 178.
8. Mithen, p. 10 and 203. Peterson and Goodall p. 25. Leakey (1992); p. 94 has a gorilla separation date of 9.5 m.y.a. and an ape date of 7.5. Relethford (textbook) p. 260 has the same split date of 7.5. Angela p. 42 has African rift occur 10 m.y.a. and anthropoid bipedalism p. 44 occur b/t 5 and 7 m.y.a. and this anatomical structural development synchronizes with human and ape divergence. Potts p. 77 uses the same time frame. Ruse p.120 places the break late at 5 m.y.a. and he presents that humanity is closer to ape than dog is to fox.
9. Lewin (1997), p. 165.
10. *Ibid.*, p. 166.
11. On HERV-K see Svitil's article titled "Did Viruses make Us Human" in *Discover* and on FOXP2 see Wade's article in *New York Times* titled "Insight into Human-Chimp Differences."

Chapter Ten

Black Persistency

THE UNBEARABLE BLACKNESS OF ONTOLOGY

In the natural order of things all cultures must uphold a formulated ancestral beauty that functions within a people's own respective ancient past. All cultures, nationalities, ethnicities, subspecies, self-conceptualized groups of people customarily propound an ideological positivity concerning ancestry that enables them to bring about further cohesive and self-re-*culturalized* victories. A strong culture must obtain a self-envisioned past that bestows cultural perseverance where the people believe that they have acted upon obstacles rather than seeming to be acted upon by outside proponents and where they interminably work at not seeming unhistoric. It is a culture's self-adulation and positive and esteemed reflection that help precipitate the much-needed strong heritage foundation.

In continuance with this extensive exegesis and scholarly endeavor against what I call the forever endurable white construct of an ever-insurmountable intellectualism that always seems to return to the solidified black/white dichotomy. The intellectualism inherently maintains a possessive past. From the beginnings of intellectual perceptions about worldly origins, Western reflections about an idea of black origins remained inconceivable and at certain times even abominable. A black origin endures as a mystifiable origin that never pinpoints a transcendent vector and/or victor. In early modernity the little Native American and the indigenous African were placed at the boundaries of civilization and had been rationally perceived as remnants of humanity at its most primordial and beast-like stages. Primitivism had been referenced throughout the ages. Primitivism had been regarded from the ever upgradeable and modernizing white conscious civilization. Black from white where white maintains a dominant vision in a white empowering spectrum is permissible. Black lines where black is closer to the beast than white is mentionable. White moving away from primitivism, as its ascent is forever useful is acceptable. And yet, what do we make of the portrayal of the black wild creature still toiling in its own protosocializing subcivilization with its own humanly social creativities still lurking in an overall world grown smaller than ever before?

I begin this part of the continued enquiry with a preliminary question. Why did traditional Black Nationalist and revisionist historicism, dating back within modernity to Marcus Garvey and the Pan-Africanist movement, make attacks against European allusions of a nonblack world civilization? Why did centrality-in-African movement build a black heritage in the fashion that we find? It was during the turbulent 1960s that we find the beginnings of the commodization of a historical revisionism on a black past, a black ancestry where an obstinate black power rose from the ultimate demands requested by a more responsive, a more attentive, and a more supposedly liberated black American audience. Black independent nationalism needed to exist more so then in the 1960s than ever before because biased perceptions heavily weighed down upon a construed and then still perceived ahistorical and disenfranchised group.

What do we make of what at one time had been referred to as the divided subhuman species or human subspecies or rather the commonly used term of "black race"? In particular what do we make of the reformulated and postcolonial American divide? How are divisions still recreated today? What do we make of binary and polar extremes that are derived from them? With the centrality in all things African, for example, we have argued that the "black man" had existed for millions and millions of years before the "white man" ever appeared. Darkness before there was light, blackness before whiteness, how *apropos*. In the 1960s black nationalists have proudly reasoned that prehistoric humanity had been black because the originating single human being began in a place reclaimed and renamed openly as black Africa. Centrality in all things African has argued that it was all because of the greatness of the "black man" of the fertile Nile where primordial civilization had been truly created. They have further argued that it was the "black man's" doing that spurred on the effectiveness that we see in the first developments of prehistoric humanity's survival, i.e., a persistency that ultimately led the way from proto-village to ancient society. Those centralized in all things African are countering a Western world, that symbolically misconstrues nonwhiteness and otherness and that now currently prevails with other derivatives not only of a white/black dichotomy (or white/nonwhite dichotomy), but also of a divisive and still disuniting world, i.e. it is the continuum endeavoring of a Westernizing world that has perpetually created and recreated perspectives about what white is not.

SCIENTOLOGY OF THE RACIALIZING BELIEF SYSTEM

Consequentially modern American history, the 1960s, helps to elaborate a point about the social effects of racialization. For the moment, let us look at the American layperson's perceptions during an American historical moment of turmoil: the civil strife of the 1960s. Long ago in the tumultuous times of active citizenry on 3 September 1962, a federal district court ordered the University of Mississippi to admit James Meredith, a newly admitted African American student. Ole Miss would be one of the first of many other institutions to come up to the changing times and it was not about to give in so easily. On the same exact day that the court's decision came down, the Governor of Mississippi, Ross Barnett, a staunch segregationist, went on statewide television to make a statement against the federal court decision. In order to maintain Barnett's constituency he expounded white racial pride by stating, "[t]here is no case in history where the Caucasian race has survived social integration..."[1] Some institutional representatives have believed that integration has only led to the demise of society. We can assess from American history that such thoughts against human equality across varying cultures was upheld no matter how socially injurious to a denied group.

Here is another example that occurred just two years and four months after the Ole Miss incident in Selma, Alabama. On 2 January 1965 the great late Rev. Dr. Martin Luther King spoke at Brown's Chapel African Methodist Episcopal Church in an attempt to get more African Americans to vote. After the church services reporters had flocked to the A.M.E. Church to cover one of King's most influential speeches, and immediately they went on to ask the white officials who were also present why was it that so few blacks were registered in Selma. Sheriff Clark responded and said that it was "largely because of their mental I.Q." And another white official, Judge Hare, spoke to another reporter and said,

> You see, most of your Selma Negroes are descended from the Ebo and Angola tribes of Africa. You could never teach or trust an Ebo back in slave days and even today I can spot their tribal characteristics. They have protruding heels, for instance.[2]

How is it then that these two Southern white American officials living in the 1960s came to formulate these ideas about African Americans? Were they prior anthropologists or social scientists expressing credible sources? Did they seem particularly believable to a white America? Yes.

Historically speaking, perceptions about the term *race* have always been quite harmful. It is these kinds of held *racialized* beliefs exampled here by Judge Hare and Governor Barnett (two supposedly rational thinking professionals of their times who held powerful positions while working for the public) and two validating figures that have helped to further maintain the destructive inequalities throughout the struggle of the 1960s. These assumptions (one could say) are referred to here as having "anthropological meaning" (or manifestations of a social construct) and that involve a traditional sense of anthropology. Although this sense comes from laypersons one could add that they are being "scientological" and one could further also add that the notions maintained leads a life and is self-legitimized and infuses an idea about otherness and specifically about blackness. This arbitrarily chosen example from the racially based civil strife of the 1960s is presented here to help further make an assessment about the contemporary common European American and his/her everyday use of science to adjudicate human demarcations between the white and "the other." Is science to blame for the stance taken by the two white officials? Perhaps we should answer "no" because there are also other numerous unmentioned factors involved. But we cannot deny that today in the twenty-first century as in the past, Westernizing science not only helps in categorizing almost everything, but also helps in validating qualitatively too and in reproducing assessments about nonwhiteness.

Can we now state that the days of biased public officials are far-gone? Have we become more humane to our fellow people since the 1960s? According to Hollinger we have gone from anti-racist tactics of yesterday to the "ethno-racial blocs" of the present.[3] We have moved from a triangle form of separation (dated 1955) Protestant, Catholic, and Jew, within an all-white inner self-containing divide (blacks and others as the generic category of colored excluded), to a pentagonal separation of Asian Americans, African Americans, Indigenous (Native Americans), Hispanic Americans, and White.[4] Why can we not just be Americans? Why must we be hyphenated? The imperator of present day African-American intellectualism Henry Louis Gates had once advised that the problem with America is the hyphen. He had cautioned and had instructed America to take the emphasis out of the hyphen, and so the problem with America and the West for that matter is divisiveness and its abusive use that interminably accrues in a hyphenated America. In America as with most of the highly advanced industrialized world and its imperative everyday use of science, we have gone to categorize American subnationalities. Hollinger noted the problem when he states that "conflating race is part of the problem and not the solution," and I would also add that perceived descents becomes an inherent factor that must be considered as a critical ideal that has disharmonized our social existence.[5] Hollinger offered multiple solutions and explicates in a multi-culti stance, but here we will ask is science also to blame?

How is it that we can assign a color to a people? When we attach such melanin attributes how is it that we can choose to make a people part of an enclosed group merely by calling a group of existing people "Black" for example? How is it that a group of people in this heavily miscegenated and now inter-"*racially*" and sexualized contemporary era still be labeled Black, White, Asian, and Hispanic (the latter is not even a color but rather a language that one could add helps to devise a parameter even geographically as Latin which was devised by the British)? For this twenty-first century multicolorful America, there are no in-betweens. There are no intermediates. We have held the fossil remains mostly found in Africa as being near human and human and as not having any held color attributes such as we customarily attach to colorized ethnicities and moreover to even ourselves today.

BLACK NEO-ONTOLOGIES

In this enquiry, blackness may be regarded and considered as an African centered view. In this presentation on prehistory, those centered on Africa greatly differ and see a very monoracial ruling past. They would argue that "Blacks" have existed thousands and thousands of years before any whites can be found. All australopithecines dated 2.5 m.y.a. and perhaps even its precursor *Ardipithecus ramidus*, (again as I stated, perhaps the first hominid and the best intermediate we have to date) dated to about 4.4 m.y.a. or earlier, would be considered not only autochthonously African, but also, in the bipolarizing and dichotomous African and European intellectualized realm, as black. If we anachronistically contemporize and expound imaginary racialistic skin tones on to these specimens what would they be? Should they remain imperceptible in the fossil record? Or should we reconsider and geographically rediscover these as African hominids? Could we be capable of rediscovering them as African nonetheless even if they still fall within a prehistoric and preracialized world?

Certain Black nationalists in the past did refer to the origin of blackness and the origin of "man" as existing within one and the same locality. This blackness is where all others have derived; all had come from Mother Africa. The same Mother Africa that brought us the first fruit of life and as we have ascended from Black Mother Africa in time we have arrived at a different kind of superiority, a superiority that has derived also from an unwanted Mother Africa. From prehistory, we can interpret that the predominance of the australopithecine's early provenience has not brought on world dominance. Those centered on Africa counter this white exclusivity of the past or contend with this eurocentric propounding of a black gainlessness despite even the European thought of a African premier-ing prevalence. Those centralizing in all things African counter statements that express African subjugation despite even presumed demographic and/or notions of an ecological "r" rather than "k" rate of reproduction. In a supposedly black/white or nonwhite/white constructed world nonwhiteness inevitably would logically outnumber white.

Nevertheless, working within constructs blackness becomes a scientific European manufactured "race" that forever changes to another scientific human-made aesthetic. Black is a concept just as white, Asian, Latinos and Arabs, and etc. etc. etc., where all become part of a device that helps us to create insurmountable hatreds that further lead to terrible physical as well as mental forms of stereo-typified genocides. As the white *anthropos* searches and re-searches to find deeper understandings of the supposed human self, s/he finds more and more categories for nonwhite males and females; he finds more labels to help those other evil forces better maintain Olympian order. As those centralized in all things African find more and more counter-creative avenues to debunk and debase white deceptions of the world, those centered on all things African will find that that which they find disgusting and might be re-energized by their own work as they too replicate and replicate as they contend with a cyclic scientific European thinking person (now self-categorized as the Panhuman) who further reinvents himself in the same old traditional anti-African (and European based) critiques. What will this continued process ultimately make of the African [European deflecting] scholar?

In an almost *ex nihil*-istic fashion one can assert that something can appear from a fundamental mixture such as from dust and water. From the nothingness, we see the black space that is overwhelmingly expansive. This survey asserts now that white comes from black as the creationist God states, in the *Old Testament*, *Genesis 1:3*, "Let there be light!" and thus all now know that before whiteness there was universal darkness.[6] The entire world began from darkness and all must understand that all things come from the black as the black continues to remain in every single one of us. This is my point indeed!

This enquiry cannot entirely profess that the fossil remains are African in the contemporized sense of Africanness. Most prehistoric environmental geologists would argue that the world is forever changing. The Africa of today may not have been the Africa of let us say 4.4 m.y.a. or 2.5 m.y.a. Change is always inevitable. The African australopithecines of the prehistoric yesterdays were reaching forward. The African australopithecines worked on surviving consistently for over a million years. An African entity strove to change, and to work on surviving until another yet necessitated morphology arrived. The destined change would have produced a greater being than the long-awaited, modern African. The multifaceted African persisted in the past and helped to precipitate further advancing forms. There can be no doubt that it had all been because of an African.

There had been no problem with calling "gray eyed" Athena, Athena the Great Western Goddess of Might, War, City, Council, Worker and nurturer of children, daughter of Zeus, a divine child, and an androgynous and celibate figure, which sprung from the intellect of the Great Father. This pristine figure bestowed a great deal to Civilization and was an indestructible Olympic descendant who had been presupposed as the heir to Zeus's throne. Her birth from the head of Zeus at Lake Tritonis in Africa made her African by today's international standards and yet her origins had always remained ambiguous.[7] Despite her connection to other African native goddesses throughout preHellenic and Hellenic times, her ethnicity remained doubtful. A problem arises when that very same goddess named Athena transforms and in 1987 C.E. and is proclaimed "Black." The big debate with a Black Athena was not the self-attestation of an African (or more properly given Benalian analysis Semitic) heritage of our great civilizational existence, but rather the conflict arose when we came to define ourselves as stemming from something of a certain nontraditional and perceived insignificant nonwhiteness. The problem was that Western Civilization could not be conceived as deriving from blackness. The problem still remains that we, civilized human beings, had derived from the same unwanted blackness.

Blackness has always been perceived as the antithesis of whiteness, any child can perceive this. Euroscience has to re-mystify its most simple and obvious originality. Euroscience had to discover bones far off non-African lands; "Beijing Man" in Zhoukouchan, China (correctly referred to as *Choi K'ou Tien*) had been proclaimed the original human. Not far back into scholarly history Europeans had once held a consensus about an Asian hominid origin. Euroscience had to also hold up high the Java man discovery from Indonesia and also hold up even the less unwanted Neanderthals from Europe, which all helped to further refrain from maintaining that painful African reality.

Please do not get the enquiry wrong, the black had been noted. The black long ago had been known and categorized as *Afer*. Carl von Linne or *Carolus Linnaeus*, back in 1758, a Swedish botanist/naturalist who devised the Linnaean Hierarchy by his tenth edition of the *Systema Naturae*, which contained all kinds of profound inferences, had subliminally taxonomized our divisively human evolutionary passage through time. *Linnaeus* a renowned scholar from The University categorized two *Homo genera*, (1) *Homo sapiens* (human) and (2) *Homo troglodytis* (anthropoid apes) and from the former he made four subspecies of humanity: (1) *europaeus*, (2) *afer*, (3) *asiaticus*, and (4) *americanus*. From that moment in a modern sense it can be presented that humanity becomes well ordered. Forget the expansive array of what may be perceived as an order based on deep rooted and natural selective chance expansively in motion. What this enquiry now goes to describe are godlike scientific processes with names such as the modern synthesis, natural selection, adaptation, punctuated equilibrium, exaptation, adaptation, habitat tracking, species sorting, population isolation, and so, and so, and so. Forget all of Nature's well-ordered chaos with multiple trajectories all half-chance based, more or less. Forget about a world viewed in its well-disordered flux perpetually mixing and remixing to bring about yet other formerly diversified forms and instead let us traditionalize and tend towards a claimable and autonomous purity.

Did *Linnaeus* obtain the divine right to square peg and box and denaturalize rounded existences? Scientific white intellectual must remember that,

> [s]cience is not merely a discovery of pre-existent facts: it is also, and more importantly, a creation of something new. It is just as creative as art, though in a different way. Scientific laws are not something existing from eternity in their or in the mind of God, waiting to be discovered by man: they, did not exist before men of science formulated them. The same is true of scientific concepts, like atom, electrical potential, or evolution. [8]

Scientific intellectuals create all of what science produces. Scientific European derived intellectual has created evolution and has created the concept of "races"—all are constructed divisions to better instill our comprehension of otherwise mystical happenings. Paleontologists are creative like those of the University of Uppsala, Sweden who climbed over Mongolian rocks to get to the mysterious huge dragon bones and to get to the fossilized mammalian teeth which at one time to all did not attract as much attention until the scientific white man proclaims it part of the beginnings of humanity and slaps a label on it and refers to it as Peking "Man," *Sinanthropus*.

Races, according to a German scholar, Franz Weidenreich, could be traced back very deeply in the fossil record and at certain geologic times; they have even retained their evolutionary centers, which directly relate to our races today. Weidenreich believed that there were certain degrees of separation to *Homo Soloensis*, a propped up eastern prehistoric "man" that soon was regarded as the *original* "man" found near the Solo River located in central Java. And yet another creative scientist, and mythic creator, Eugene Dubois, a young Dutch anatomist and physician back in 1887 with a gang of convicts worked at an idea. The East as this enquiry has mentioned was where it was thought to have all begun. The East was where it must all begin Eugene staunchly held and he agreed with another great creator Harvard's own Haeckel who established the hypothesis of a Southeast Asian origin where "the link" could *only* be.

This Eastern idea held by many great and educated thinkers of course disregarded the Darwinian black African origin belief. Again, it could not have been black Africa. And so, Dubois, in a sense a Darwinian and also in a paradoxical sense a non-Darwinian believer, searched and found the supposedly self-proclaiming "missing link" then classified as *Pithecanthropus*, "Ape-human," *erectus*, "upright walker," neither ape nor human, but both. Original "man" was maintained in what has been described as the Trinil skullcap of 900 cubic centimeters and Dubois believed the stature of his find to be somewhat even similar to modern Europeans. He had found the link and not just some giant gibbon.[9] Thus, as it was customarily held in the 1800s and early 1900s, that just as the sun rises in the East so too must "Man" begin in the East and it can be added that the proof would remain forever quite osseous and extant. As of today, we are still held to the strongly exonerative and undying belief that all things must rise from one single designated point.

The blackness must always remain denied. How could we come from you dark face of originality? This enquiry now turns to a film that expresses a point about "scientological" or rather "anthropological beliefs." One of the last few lines in the 1970s fifth film of a dramatic series on talking and walking apes, which was titled "Conquest of the Planet of the Apes," had made a prophetic statement that alludes to the concept of the original human. A frightened and glassy eyed man yells back, "We have always denied our ancestry from you because it is the wild animal in us that we have always repressed!" The "wild animal" referred to here in this film by the leader of the training and retention center for conforming servant apes is a diabolically marked and conscious talking ape. The "wild animal" is a dark and hairy ape, a black ape. In the riveting conclusion to this very apocalyptic scene in the end of the film, a frightened white human leader speaks and he glares with deep intensive scorn at the several bobbing beady-eyed black apes standing in the background. While the leader spits and spews the rationale behind withholding humanity's connected past the camera shoots back and forth from white man to black ape to black man to black ape and back to the glaring white man. It seems that here modern intellectual finally confronts what could be perceived as his long past and prehistoric australopithecine brother. Here time is warped and the modern intellectual must come to understand where humanity comes from. Modern humanity will always be reminded of their so-called wild and disordered past.

Modern European humanity has always perceived itself to be held back by its identification of a black inner self. Science has always wanted to repress it, and yet in the dark crevice of white existence lays the blackness, a blackness always wanting to be rediscovered and re-revealed. And yes, after each conflictive revolving time in European derived intellectual's advancement, there lies an associative periodic sequence. Inevitably a black prehistoric humanity is re-denied, re-unacknowledged, put back into the pre-silenced dark crevice of the origins of world civilization. Black Athena was not about the blackening of the Greeks, the blackening of the Egyptians, the blackening of civilization, all deriving its perpetuity from a hidden and purposively concealed blackness, it was more. It was more than the title itself, which gave a jolt; it was more than what Bernalian diacritical analysis tried to do, which made the real mark in scholarship. It was awareness of the black/white divided-self that really made a mark.

In this book, the enquiry has gone back further to the beginnings of the human, further back than just to the blackening of Egyptians and proto-Greeks, back further than to the blackening of even the Hebraic peoples. This enquiry has blackened even the skulls, which because of their whiteness have maintained Western intellectual's handhold-ability. Paleo-ontologists have grasped the ossified forms that simply can forever retain their whiteness. Bones are beautifully and predominately white at first, but then they become yellow with age and still we notate the whiteness.

There is only one color exception for the blue-black cranium KNM-WT 17000, commonly referred to as "Black Skull," one of the earliest robust australopithecines found in 1984, that was located 5 to 10 kilometers (3 to 6 miles) inland from the western shore of Lake Turkana, Kenya, that dates to around 2.5 m.y.a. and which has remained unlinked to *afarensis* or *africanus*, subliminally perhaps because of its heavily dark pigmented surface which derived from the manganese-rich sediments in which it was first found. It sustains a darkened surface that will remind anyone of color and tones--color that unfortunately makes us most times in this present world what we are. Not only its color, but also its cranial small size and its retention of some primitive features, and slightly early dated than the earliest *australopithecus bosei* helps to separate and disconnect this hominid specimen from entering the evolving lines of a unified humanity.

So researchers now place it in its own category and they call it *Australopithecus aethiopicus* because it comes between *afarensis* and *boisei*. Also, tragically enough, it belongs in the *robustus* line that later leads to an evolutionary dead-end. More interesting in regards to this "black skull" is that it lived between 3 and 2 m.y.a. a time range that can be considered the dark ages of hominid evolution for anthropology finds very little fossil remains throughout this period.[10] Also, having evolved by 2.6 m.y.a. this is the period when African climatic changes are believed to have precipitated various kinds of extinctions and speciation as the present arid environment began and brought about a split between robust and gracile australopithcines.[11] Some would consider *aethiopicus* as precursor to *bosei* in the eastern African region as *africanus* precursored *robustus* in the southern African region.

Nonetheless, white bones are not maintained in the reticent black crevice and they no longer withhold their barbaric, primitive, prehistoric or even black-racialized- ontogeny. Physical anthropologists have held them like prized possessions under lock and key and like the Egyptian priests who were the only ones allowed to read and interpret hieroglyphs (sacred writings) or like Renaissance alchemists with their esoteric and very influential cryptic observations, they have read and interpreted ancestry and they have asserted destinies and passages of paved time in a possessing past in order to create and, or yes, recreate the present belief system of a divisive human species. Anachronistically, if only we could un-*racialize* in order to clear up and retain a more precise vision in our twenty-first century time continuum and in order to obtain a better present with less refractions. Looking into the past will always be refractory.

UNYIELDING INTERCONNECTIVITY

This enquiry has gone on about blackness a great deal and has not thoroughly claimed what it is that the deconstruction purports. At this juncture, the enquiry continues to express a contradictory understanding and endures with a diachronological and archaeological analysis of the prehistoric pre-human-to-human trajectory. This analysis points out the overall human tendencies toward spreading and the overwhelming human propensity to remain connected with each other. This enquiry merely sustains that there can never be an encapsulated separatist and entirely divided entity that can progress because prehistoric pre-human and human existence imaginatively unacknowledged and scholarly preconceived have always relationally maintained each within their own respective continuum of time and space. As this enquiry withstands to forge ahead, the effort turns to the early hominids and lead up to the early developments of what can be referred to as a prehistoric society.

Looking backwards and confronting what we see takes great strength. To look back and to explain what one sees without bending and without temerity of the staunch paradigmatic envisioning sciences involves an unrelinquishable endurance. We are not solipsistically red, black, white, yellow or brown, but interconnected and all interchangeably changing as we come to be more enriched in an interminably diversified future. It is how we make our past that truly creates our present. There can be no disputing that the record of the past is incorporated into the soul of a people; the past forms an essential part of our social identity. And so, this enquiry will form a multiple and meshing and yet colorful world where Elysian and harmful separatisms are not allowed.

NOTES

1. Williams, p. 215.
2. Ibid, p. 258.
3. Ibid, p. 85– 86.
4. Ibid, p. 23– 24 and see also the U.S. Census Report 2000.
5. Ibid, p. 38–39.
6. *The New American Bible.*
7. Rose, H.J. p. 109.
8. Huxley, p. 100.

9. Brace, p. 23, states that an elderly Dubois had recanted and subsequently believed his find to be just that a giant gibbon. Brace cites Dubois, I. (1935).

10. Johanson and Edgar (1996), p. 152.

11. Ibid, p. 28 who depends on Elizabeth Vrba's "turnover pulse hypothesis."

Chapter Eleven

Africanic Homodization

AUSTRALOPITHECINE APARTHEIDS

Australopithecus, the revelational "southern ape" labeled as such for that is where the first of its kind had been identified, in the southern parts of Africa, was the name given to the foremost discovered member of a series of fossils of hominids, which were closely related to developing human beings and primarily found in South Africa back in the early twentieth century. Since the very first discovery of its kind by an Australian named Raymond Arthur Dart who trained as a medical studies academic and who graduated from University of Queensland and who subsequently went to England to work as an assistant to a fellow Australian neuroanatomist, Grafton Elliot Smith, but who was somewhat rejected and thus was sent to South Africa to University of Witwaterstrand to fill the position of professor of anatomy. It was Raymond Dart who in 1924 in Johannesburg, South Africa, revealed to the world what had been found at what has been referred to as the Taung site. In South Africa there began a categorization of forms of hominid species titled *Australopithecus*.[1] This term, *Australopithecus*, soon began to take precedence over a variety of ape-like skeletal remains and other similar kinds of hominid remains which have been found at numerous places in the southern parts and as well as the eastern parts of Africa. One preliminary site that was worked on back in the early twentieth century was the Taung site. *Taung* is a South African local word, which means the place of *Tau*, the place of the Lion. Dart argued that his newly discovered find be considered as a humanlike ape. He wanted the form to be considered as a *Homo-simiadae* form (just another word for what has been considered the human-ape grouping).

The little skull found by the Australian professor, i.e., Raymond Dart, was immensely provoking. The "Taung Boy" discovery had changed the perception of humanity forever. It was as critical a discovery as Copernican heliocentricity, Mendelian hereditable peas, or Watson and Crick's double helix, or even better yet as stupendous a discovery as the astronomical realization that the universe is expanding and that everything around us is in orderly motion. Dart's 1925 article had revolutionized our world. The idea of missing links first was of course rejected by an extremely too stagnant nineteenth century paradigmatic science and this would always be the case when scholars gather around each other and restrict themselves to a too small isolated group of similarly thinking scientists. An African origin could not possibly have been our human's ancestral home. Europe, or Asia definitely yes, would be the prime venue for origins of humanity, but certainly not wild Africa, where all forms customarily seem overly savage and too fragmented.

Around the same time right before the Taung Boy's discovery, back in 1922, at a very different location far from Africa, there was another formerly named creation, which was immediately called *Hesperopithecus haroldcooki*. It was considered a western versioned extinct pithecine and its classification had been made merely from a discovery of a sole and singular molar. It was presented to the world by Henry Fairfield Osborn, the same person who inspired the American Museum of Natural History to conduct an expedition into the ground of China to find the then so adamantly believed "Dawn Man," i.e., the "Man from where the sun rises." Harold J. Cook, an American geologist, had found the singular tooth in the Snake Creek fossil beds of Nebraska. Soon after its hopeful discovery more searches ensued in the Snake Creek site and they yielded more worn down teeth, but finally this time, unfortunately for the great white creators, it was ultimately revealed that all the newly discovered teeth belonged to a jaw of an extinct wild pig.[2] Dismayingly and reluctantly enough, the American specimen had to be released and excluded from furthering the European construct. Using the American discovery as the long sought after place of origin for prehistoric "American Man" could not stand.

There were many wishful attempts at trying to find ape-human specimens outside of Africa at the turn and beginning of the twentieth century. There were other locations, other than Africa, that were assumed to have been birthplaces of the originating present human. There are still other sites even now being excavated where out-of-African finds are direly sought. But saddening enough for white constructions on origins all that we have are African pithecines that date until around the one million year mark and earlier, a critical time for the ever transforming humanoid process as hominids further went on to evolve into present humans.

All that we have are the African australopithecines that date between the last half of the late Miocene epoch (5.3 m.y.a) and the beginning of the Pleistocene epoch (1.6. m.y.a.). It is between the end of the Miocene or the late Miocene epoch and the late Pliocene epoch that we begin to first find australopithecines. In the archaeological record as early as the Pliocene epoch that we begin to find the established forms of *Australopithecus*, which start to date back to between 4.2 and 3.9 million years ago. One of the oldest australopithecine that we have is found at Aramis, (Middle Awash) Ethiopia. It has been labeled *Australopithecus ramidus* (which makes use of the local word in Afar language, *ramid*, for "root") and it came from Pliocene deposits that are dated to 4.4 m.y.a. *A. ramidus* has been believed to be the "root" species of all later hominids.[3] It is also believed that *Australopithecus ramidus* existed before the expansion of later hominids into the grassland regions.[4] Some paleontologists like Tim White have given this taxon a new generic name of *Ardipithecus*.[5] *Australopithecus ramidus* is smaller than typical *Australopithecus afarensis* forms.

Moreover, in regards to the australopithecine fossil evidence, some scholars find in them a key fundamental representation of temporal forms that display to us the slow transformational process that has supposedly led its way toward our upright and standing *Homo erectus* and then on to modern *Homo sapiens*. Despite all the sensationalistic hoopla by the media of "man comes from ape" stories, we find that most paleontologists come to agree that the australopithecines are a decisive unique-transmorphological link between fossilized apes and fossilized proto-humans. Some scholars have even come to display these forms in humanistic fashion on the covers of their books.[6] These fossilized hominids have become not only the main objective for the interminable search to find what forms transitionally precipitated further change toward humanity, but also they are bearers of information about how it was that "we" existed as "we" did for over several million years. The "we" here of course is inherent in the argument that australopithecines or hominids inclusively helped to formulate humanity throughout specific prehistoric periods on earth.

Again, there are two kinds of major groups of African regional sites where australopithecines are found: (1) the South Africa country and (2) the East African countries of Tanzania, Kenya, and Ethiopia. As stated above the South African australopithecines all began with Dart's Taung child's skull.

AUSTRALOPITHECINES: BOTH BIG AND SMALL

These fossils were categorized as *africanus* types or otherwise known as gracile forms, and/or they were perceived as robust. The references of gracile and robust are useful because the two described subgroups are different in size but seem as being closely connected. Some have even gone on to argue that the differing forms are due to a widely extensive sexual dimorphism.[7]

Most researchers would agree that there is a distinct difference between gracile and robust forms. This difference can visibly be inferred from the robust forms with the absence of a forehead, an enlarged great post orbital constrition to accommodate a large temporalis muscle, a sagittal crest, and large browridges, these particular cranial traits add up to powerful masticatory activity perhaps body weight and strength. These robust ape-like forms once referred to as "nutcrackers" were huge and they were created to serve a purpose, i.e. survive, as with all animals in our planet earth. The ruggedness of the robust forms is absent in gracile types, according to Robinson the physiological disparity reflects a difference in diet and behavior, gracile is a meat eater and omnivorous, and the robust forms are tough vegetarian eaters who were subsisting on such things as roots, tubers and bulbs.[8] Robinson reclassifed "gracile" as *Homo africanus* because he came to see them more and more as slightly further advanced to humanness than robust forms. He called them *africanus* and this would have alluded to our *A. africanus* titled forms who as of yet we must remember have body sizes that apparently did not differ much between *A. africanus* and *A. robustus.*[9]

What some have customarily come to argue is that the gracile and robust forms perhaps may not be the result of functional and biological differences, but that the results and differences that we see belong to similar animals with varying body sizes and physical features as we commonly find when we compare an Eastern European Slav with a Guatamalan Native American from a Chiapas village. Robust could be "blow up" versions of gracile. Perhaps they may have morphological, behavioral and ecological differences, but they are within the same animal or form, one perhaps extremely varying and multiple form.[10] There are also some that would argue and believe in a single species hypothesis such as that cited by Conroy who cites Wolpoff's (1971) competitive exclusion theory where Wolpoff turns to living gorillas.[11] It was Pilbeam and Gould who argued that *africanus*, *robustus*, and *boisei* were the same and they came to assert this from the examination done in a study of brain size versus body size within the hominids in question. It is believed that the differences are as great as even those of the pygmie-chimp, chimp, and gorilla as it was produced from an allometry analysis.[12]

What we again could be seeing is the clustering and grouping of various forms and in order to construct a logical and a sequentialized progression of varying forms in order to show that there had been no mixing, just as there had been no miscegenation ever. Miscegenation had been frowned upon during the seventeenth century and the American colonial era.[13] According to Sigmund Freud the oldest and strongest known taboos within most early societies seemed to have strictly prohibited two things (1) that there could be no incest, marriage must always be "exogamous," that is outside the immediate family or clan, and (2) that there was no killing or eating of the totem animal except for certain ceremonial occasions.

These were rules that everyone wanted to keep that was why they were made not to stop but instead to help the species survive by the acquirement of varying and useful attributes such as bigger bodies or smaller, more efficient and omnivorous eating systems such as those found in the gracile forms. The gracile form was just that gracile, easily accommodating to ecological conditions given the changing environment. If the cold weather had been universal or if vegetation increases become expansive the robust forms or for that matter also Neanderthal would have prospered in vegetation and nut inducive environments which would have made pervasive the robust types since they could find it better to persist, but that had just not been the case. When there is no need, Natural Selection will almost always inevitably discard that function which becomes no longer a necessity for survival.

Some scholars have even argued that we should rename the robust forms, *Paranthropus* ("next to human") and some actually assigned this title to the *boisei*, *robustus*, and *aethiopicus* forms and long ago this was the name that Broom had previously assigned to them back in 1938. Most of the australopithecines found in the South African region were found in caves. Broom had made a skull discovered in the Kromdraai Cave just 1.5 km east of Sterkfontein the type specimen (Transvaal Museum, TM 1517), which was named *Paranthropus robustus*. Since 1948 Swartkrans proved to be a richer site for *A. robustus* specimens, they have also been found in East Africa and they have also been labeled *A. boisei* (or *A. aethiopicus*). Only the South African *A. robustus* from Kromdraai, Sartkrans and Drimolen are considered truely *A. robustus*.[14]

Some could argue that there are no real differences between the *A. boisei* and *A. robustus*. The only real difference or differentiating quality is what the discoverers themselves have come to possess and have come to label in their own distinct way. The south and the east have come to maintain a scholarly created divide, which has obstinately remained held in the renewed and re-colonized sub-worlds of Africa. Researchers of the prehistoric past created their own creatures and they have not released any single one of them. The discovering or devising paleographers have toiled too hard to work for a nihilism that simplifies all things into an unknown communal scientism.

It was Robert Broom, a Glasgow University graduate, who in his 70's first came to help substantiate *Australopithecus's* existence. Broom had discovered on August 17, 1936 the first adult australopithecine that was initially called *A. transvaalensis* and then it was later changed to *Plesianthropus*.[15] It was later on, almost ten years after when Broom began the labeling of his finds in June of 1947, that he discovered a fine lower jaw, which greatly assisted in confirming the scientific perception of human-like rather than ape-like australopithecines. The discovery of teeth came to attribute a great deal of attention to australopithecines. Back in the Sterkfontein caves of South Africa, Broom also came to find very important skeletal parts such as a complete pelvis, a vertebral column, leg bone fragments, and a skull and all these various anatomical parts were used to help establish australopithcines as the long sought after and supposed hominid transitional forms that led the way to presently developed human. The same Sir Arthur Keith who had been implicated by some as a suspect in the Piltdown affair had written a letter to Broom when he had made the great South African discovery congratulating him and saying you have found what I never thought could be found that is to say that Broom had found a human-like jaw connected to an ape-like skull and this was the exact opposite of what the fabricated Piltdown Man had been.[16]

With Broom, early twentieth century men begin to understand and manufacture the proof that they needed to counter-argue that encephalization had been the final stage to human's evolutionary ascendance. It was Broom who helped to make australopithecines erect and bipedal with the clearly visible human-like dentition connected to a very small ape-sized cranium, and this of course became the needed ancestral proof to show that intermediary forms existed before *Homo* appeared. It is now commonly believed that the significance of cranial expansion is the distinctive feature of the emergence and development of solely the genus *Homo*.[17]

Although one could counter-argue that in the South African sites for the most part *A. africanus* had been replaced by populations of *A. robustus,* which had coexisted at a certain co-temporaneous period with *H. habilis* and then later with *H. erectus*. It is believed that australopithcine's existence in southern Africa spans over 2 million years. The sites, Taung, Makapansgat, Sterkfontein, Swartkrans, Kromdraai,where *A. africanus* existed first before *A. robustus* were critical sites in attesting to the long time spans. And throughout the two million years we also do find tools and fauna remains, which have led some to interpret home base habitations.

EASTSIDE AFRICANS

When we come to where a great deal of australopithecines have also been found we must turn to the East African region where we begin to find some of the oldest finds in Africa. The oldest hominids are asserted from a single mandibular fragment from the Lothagam site dated to 5.6 m.y.a. and then there is the specimens of *A. ramidus* from Aramis Ethiopia dated to about 4.4 m.y.a.[18] These specimen finds have been seen as ardipithecines because of their thin enamel and primitive dentine morphology. We also learn that Laetolian *A. anamensis* or *afarensis* walked somewhat bipedally at around 3.6 m.y.a. If we consider the Hadar, Omo, Lake Turkana and Olduvai finds we see that the australopithecine not only persisted but developed for quite some time from say 4.4 to 1 m.y.a. when they cease to exist and have even maintained contemporaneity with *H. habilis*. Given all this time of persistence we find that they have existed all between the South Africa and Chad as finds have attested to. We can also note from all the African finds that australopithecines did some traveling.

The oldest stone tools yet discovered from Africa are Oldowan Industry types from Gona, Ethiopia dated to 2.5 m.y.a. and also from Ethiopia in Omo group deposits dated to 2.4–2.3 m.y.a. quartz flakes and stone tools from Members F and G in the Shungura Formations have been found.[19] It is important to point out that these tools cannot be directly linked to a particular hominid as the specified toolmaker.[20] Yet simple tools of the Oldowan type have been used during the time of the australopithecines. Dart had always believed this to be true and Louis Leakey still by 1958 had not believed that his particular East African australopithcines were as skilled as stone-tool-holding men. Nevertheless, throughout the 1956 to 1958 excavations at the Sterkfontein caves perceptible tools had been discovered.[21]

Louis Leakey who commonly referred to australopithcines as "near-men," continually considered them as more prehistoric ape than anything else. He even went as far as to believe that "true-men" had been eating the "near-men" and this interpretation helped to affirm the logical reasoning behind finding tools beside australopithecines.[22]

However, Leakey did finally come to terms with their human-like qualities and he then came to assign to them the name *Zinjanthropus boisei* (the *Zinj* word is part Arabic for a medieval area of the East African coast. It literally means "East Africa." *Anthropos* is "human," *boisei* is a Latinated form of Leakey's very generous benefactor at the time, and thus we have "Boise's East African human").[23] According to Leakey the "Boise's East African human" (or "Nutcracker Human" as he also began to be commonly referred to by the press because of the large teeth and jaw) was a close relative of "near-human" that is "near-human" of South Africa (an australopithecine or the sometime referenced term of *Paranthropus*). "Boise's East African human" was a human in the sense that s/he was a creator of tools. Leakey believed that "*Zinj* Man" or "Boise's East African Human" was closer to human than the supposed australopithecine.[24]

It seems that when *Zinjanthropus boisei* had been found in Olduvai Gorge it soon became the common belief that the "real" missing link had been discovered. It was this find that led the discoverer to create his own devised species, and thus OH 5 was labeled *Zinjanthropus boisei*. The specimen was even paraded around all the way to America as the find that answered the greatest riddle of life; Original humanity had now been evidenced. And as it was the specimen was used and showcased on 24 November 1959 as the "missing link" even at the University of Chicago's Darwin Centennial Gala where the two grandsons of the great contributors of classification gave speeches, Sir Charles Darwin and Sir Julian Huxley.[25]

In 1959, OH 5, an Olduvai Hominid, a well-preserved cranium, was found to be quite similar to what had been found in the South African Swartkrans and Kromdraai caves, *robustus* forms. More discoveries later in 1964 and onwards of *robustus* types in the East African region confirmed this type to have coexisted in the eastern parts as well as with those that were found in the southern parts. In the East African region there were other finds that seemed a great deal more human than would otherwise have been categorized as specimens, there were some who were found with bigger brains and smaller teeth (of course these types of finds went on to be labeled as *Homo habilis*).

What also were discovered were skulls and tools on the same FLK living floor. In Bed I at Olduvai Gorge and what at first should have been human had not been found. There were no human forms found together with these tools, and so finally there was no other choice than to come to the conclusion that some kind of biotic gradualistic developmental process ensued that did not include quite as of yet the enlarged-cranial-retaining human. Bigger brain human did not make those tools and this was evident because she/he was not found anywhere around the tools, and thus what we have is a renaming of some of the various "*Zinj* Men" to the convenient category of *Australopithecus* b*oisei*. It was Phillip Tobias who later became Dart's replacement at Witwatersrand University who came to rename it *A. boisei* in *Olduvai Gorge* (1967). Despite the great deal of size variation even within the *A. boisei* forms, what we begin to come to terms with is that *Parathropus,* "near-human" is human nonetheless. What we begin to hear about what happens in the newly created story of "Man" is that *boisei* forms die out. If the forms do not die out they become like others as the sivapithecines and ramapithecines who end up in the *cul-de-sac* form of orangutans.

Nevertheless, Leakey's East African australopithecines were instrumental in assigning the intermediate forms of hominids. Yet what makes australopithecines so debatable as human forms and considered solely to be near human is that their average brain case size is between 430 and 450 cubic centimeters and this of course is quite similar to apes than to humans. Brain size is a critical factor and body size as well. The ratio of brain to body makes the australopithecines seem closer to human than ape for they increased in body size and have not remained small as with apes in these regions of Africa. There are other features that distinguish these pithecines from human and that would be the bony crest mark that we commonly find on *robustus* skulls. The sagittal crest works as an attachment for the jaw muscles so that the muscles are better structured to work the heavy grinds of nuts and plants commonly eaten by *boisei*, *robustus* and *aethiopicus*.

A feature that brings the australopithecines closer to humans than to apes (and this is in regards to the gracile for it is believed that the *robustus* forms along with the *boisei* forms unfortunately went on to become extinct) is that the teeth are not arranged in the characteristic U-shaped fashion as that of apes, but instead they lie in a more rounded shape. A key element to seeing how intermediary these australopithecines are is to see that the incisor teeth are set vertically in the jaw and that the canines are small and do not stand out in front of the other teeth and as with most apes we do not have the gaps or the *diastema* between the canines and the premolars, and also the milk teeth are similar to humans, but the rate of maturation of the teeth is said to follow that of apes more closely than they do humans.[26] When we consider the height we note that the gracile forms average about five feet (150 centimeters) in height and their weight is estimated to have been about 75 to 130 pounds (35 to 60 kilograms) and this brings them to be smaller than humans but larger than apes.

AFRICAN TOOLS

One must wonder if they were so close back then how was it that they became capable of being devised into a semi-human form and how was it that they came to maintain themselves in a social human group-like setting with a certain degree of cohesiveness. In excavations worked on by geologist Brian and Sillen at Swartkrans in deposits dated between 1 m.y.a. and 1.5 m.y.a. some 60,000 fossil animal bones had been found and from this find there had been a sample of 270 fossils that showed signs of burning. Most of the finds had been antelope bones, which were mostly burnt at no higher than 500 C. There were Oldowan stone tools and bones with cut marks and the supposed contributor to all this tool-use eating had been perhaps nine individuals of definitive *A. robustus* form, which were also found at the site. At a different time period *H. habilis* had been found at the same location, but they come at a later time and they are found without evidence of fire.[27] We must be reminded here that tool-using hominids have always been attributed to solely the earliest species of Homo forms that existed between 3 and 2 m.y.a.[28]

Yet even with the small-brain-sized, supposed halfway humanlike forms that we have found in South Africa and the sketchy finds of quasi-homebase cooking sites we also learn from the East African finds that australopithecines may have been capable of making and using tools. Most primatologists would argue that all animals one way or another can be said to use tools even if we consider the restrictions that can be placed by animal tool-use and the degree to which we find self-mentalistic nonrecognition.[29] Primatologists likeTomasello and Call have maintained that

> complex object manipulations are not frequent in the behaviour of most animal species. Racoons wash and process their food in various ways, and a number of species, from insects to sea otters, use tools in restricted contexts. But the

> primate hand is clearly more adapted for hand feeding and other manipulative activities than the appendages of virtually all nonprimate species, and some primates' behaviour with objects takes full advantage of this morphological adaptation in manipulating objects.[30]

The way that primate hands have evolved have led us to see that they are not only useful for grabbing and climbing from branch to branch, but have come to move onward to hold objects. Yet Tomasello and Call claim that nonhuman primates do not involve themselves in the complexity of relating objects to one another, one could even go further and apply the same nonhuman primatological perceptions to australopithecines and state that there is no "complex object manipulation" and that we see austalopithecines doing is truly nonhuman-like and that we are making somewhat farfetched behavioristic assertions with the southern and eastern African prehistoric stone tools that had been discovered.

Yet on the other hand the ideal and staple example given by paleontologists and primatologist alike would probably be the commonly observable activity of the chiimpanzee's termite-extraction stick use.[31] Unfortunately, primatologists are not quite certain as to how it is that these apes come to use these instruments in the human-like manner that they do. One would infer that what we see is a conceptualization, as McGrew et al. argue, when laboratory settings have shown that bonobos have realized as they went on that there was a need for stick utilization, it is contended that they did not just sit in the jungle trees and by chance came to see a stick in a hole.[32] Yet to add more to ape-human similitudinal tool-use, according to Peterson and Goodall it is believed that termite fishing is a concept that is passed on in the same way that a human-like cultural behavior would be. It may not be entirely culture in the human sense, but it is nonetheless behavior. To Peterson and Goodall this can be a learned and not entirely just an instinctual process.[33]

A great deal of materials such as tools, fauna, floral, etc., have been found beside and around hominids in the Oldowan Industries primarily found in Beds I through IV and from the start it had been assumed by Louis Leakey that archaic human and not an australopithecine would be found in the very same stratigraphic places, that is to say over 2 m.y.a. in prehistoric times. Yet in those very same places he had found a preponderance of australopithcines. Natural forces also produce flakes that look a great deal like those struck by hominids, but handaxes, arrowheads, and even scrapers are unmistakably intended tools created by hominids.[34] Various types of australopithecines have been found and along with them, there were *H. habilis* insertions, which have complicated things, specifically the answer to the question of who really made those tools.

How is it then that the pre-human comes to exist? Or rather, shall we ask how is it that the australopithcines come in multiple forms and multiple grounds with multiple tools always somewhere near? When we consider these australopithcines we must also consider that change had not occurred, all at once, prehistorically and spontaneously, but instead again we see a very amazing kind of extremely slow-moving gradualism. What the Leakeys soon discovered as they were analyzing an Oldowan Industry is that the sites had been overlapping and variably involved by multiple and contemporaneous tool users. This multiple diachronically functionalistic tool development has led some to assert that we have two primary forms of hominids that coexisted, just as when later on throughout prehistory we have Neanderthals and archaic *Homo sapiens* consequentially residing at extreme proximity.

What the Leakeys find are several types of tools varying in creativity and ingenuity. There were

Bed I: Developed Oldowan A
Bed II: Developed Oldowan B [Abrupt appearance of Acheulian]
Bed III and IV: Again advanced Oldowan B and Acheulian [As in Bed II].

Mary Leakey had contrasted the artifacts of Bed I at Olduvai Gorge with those of Bed II that lies immediately above, and which begins to form about 1.6 m.y.a. In Bed I bone remains are predominately of small mammals, birds and fish. But in Bed II we find large animals killed with depress skull fractures by throw tools, which would suggest that hominids of Bed II had an advance in stone tool technology, which according to Megarry (a prehistoric sociologist) this indicates that a more complex social organization had been at hand. Megarry tells us that the Oldowan choppers account for more than three-quarters of all tools found in Bed I, but that only for about one-third of the contents of Bed II. There were two cultural levels at hand.[35] These more advanced tools had been described as "Developed Oldowan B"and these were considered by Mary Leakey to be "bola weights" used as missiles to strike animals from a distance.[36]

According to Reader, Mary Leakey believed that both industries coexisted about "within a few hundred meters of each other on the same geological horizon and yet they remain separated and do not comingle."[37] No one has any clue as to how the Acheulian arrives there. These two tools are not unilinear in progressivity; they have coexisted for what had been over 2.5 million years. The Oldowan and the Acheulian distinction can be explained as a differing kind of creativity the kind that would require envisioning that large flakes can be knapped out of a boulder to make handaxes. This is not so difficult once one has seen it done, but what becomes the crucial point is to have contemplated the idea to initiate and to do such a thing in the first place.[38]

Acheulian handaxes become advancement forward and both their manufacture and use imply that a higher level of skill had been attained. The significant functionality of handaxes is that hominids can cut up carcasses, large or small, and this of course points out that they would have to also have been meat eaters. These tools could not be used for nothing more important than chopping up meats. This technological advancement must have led to the facility of food preparation thereby helping feed more usefully at a wider systematized scale.

But what of the meats that were cut and the bones that were chopped? Since we do not find ash fires or hearths or remnants of meat caches we must also consider that these meats were also eaten raw again since archaeologically we do not find evidence of the use of fire until about 500,000 years ago at a site far from the African continent?[39] It is believed that the Acheulian handaxes were brought in by *H. erectus* who were found to exist in Bed II levels (dated 1.2 m.y.a.).[40]

Questions still remain about prehistoric prehumanity's developmental time sequences and their continuous habitation, which have remained not so straightforward because we can see that *H. habilis*, *erectus*, and archaic *sapiens* have not moved forward in a straight ascending existential line. We have australopithecines, *H. habilis*, and *erectus* all inhabiting in what could be perceived as living simultaneously at certain junctures. As we consider the archaeological remains such as tools, we are confounded as to how they are found in the Bed II levels. Remember that *Zinj* finds (*A. boisei* and *robustus* forms) and *H. habilis* and *erectus* lived roughly around and within closely connected time frames and also remember that all three generalized forms have varying brain sizes disregarding the ideal cranial rubicon of 700 to 800 cc. Also, if we consider, in a prehistoric chronological sense, examples taken from the respective dates of Bed I 1.9. m.y.a. and Bed II 1.2 m.y.a. we would have come to travel a very short distance of time relative to the evolutionary time scale presumed for the trajectory from prehumanity to humanity.

The mere fact that varying forms have been discovered and have been discovered using tools tells us that proto-civilizational existence perhaps within multiple and short isolated time-frames and among multiple hominid forms in defined regions had already been moving onwards towards its way to yet other variegated and coexisting future historic developments. Perhaps we are right to believe as when "*Zinj*" finds had been found that the Oldowan industry is a revelation that nearly two million years ago the social structures of African humanity had already been created and that the idea that African humanity had already maintained culturally enhancing social groupings.[41]

NOTES

1. Dart titled his find in a *Nature* article on Feb. 7th 1925 as *Australopithecus africanus*, "Southern Ape of Africa."
2. Reader, p. 110.

3. Conroy, p. 151.
4. Conroy, p. 152.
5. Conroy, p. 184.
6. See covers and illustrations in any of the Johanson and Leakey books as prime examples. Also, there are the 1970s movies series of "Planet of the Apes" which the original film script and idea came from a book written by a French anthropologist believing in perceptions about prehuman to human morphic transitions.
7. See Kimbel et al. A large *A. Afarensis* cranium from Hadar, Ethiopia dated to about 3 m.y.a. has been discovered and this could break up the robust and gracile (typically held) dichotomy. See also Conroy pp. 188-191 for a short synopsis of sexual dimorphism.
8. See dentition analysis of Robinson (1954) cited by Gamble (1993) p. 68.
9. Conroy, p. 221.
10. See Conroy p. 251 who queries Robinson's traditionalized assertions.
11. Conroy, p. 251.
12. See illustrations in Conroy, p. 252.
13. Wolpoff presents the idea that humanity had always strove to find an outsider to make love to. Also, see incest taboos in primitive cultures like Trobianders and their method for dealing with outside clans. Megarry's last chapter makes use of Levi-Straussian tribal portraitures and supports this theory about mating outsiders.
14. Conroy, p. 193.
15. Conroy, p. 137.
16. Reader p. 130. See also Spencer and Walsh.
17. Toth and Schick p. 18–19. But also see Noble and Davidson p. 34 who contrarily point out that brain size is not a sufficient indicator for establishing human behavior, human activity has occurred unnecessarily without specific enlarged cranial capacities and this is of course precursored by Broom.
18. Conroy, p. 151 and 170.
19. Conroy, p. 154–155.
20. Conroy, p. 155.
21. Reader, p. 153.
22. Reader, p. 155.
23. Ben Jochannan argued that *zinjanthropus* as a name adds some pejorativeness to the notion of an intergrading humanity primarily when connected to a people from the East African region. Ben Jochannan also points out notions of "white" formulated departure of this group from an African prehumanity, see p. 95.
24. Reader, p. 182.
25. *Ibid* p. 158–159.
26. See Conroy figures 3.3 and 3.4 for a comparative analysis on p. 88. Also see Conroy's figure 5.23 for lateral view of proximal pedal (toe) phlanges from the third toe that Conroy used to present differences anatomical differences on p. 218.
27. Gamble (1993) p. 70 who cites both Brian and Sillen and also Gowlett for another 1.4. m.y.a. *A. robustus* fire using site at Chesowanja, Kenya and Gamble using Sussman also asserts that *A. robustus* had been very capable of manufacturing tools (ibid).
28. Megarry p.157. Also Megarry asserts that the first stone tools will unlikely be positively identified, and thus there is no originated tool. p. 165.
29. Tomasello and Call p. 70.
30. Ibid. p. 70.
31. Ibid. p. 72.
32. McGrew, p. 179.
33. Peterson and Goodall p. 35. Also see ibid p. 31–33 where they go over the implementation of tool-use and primates and argue that they have observed even tool preparation for termite mound extraction miles away.
34. Whittaker, p. 17.
35. P. 196.
36. Ibid p. 197.
37. Reader, p. 177.

38. Consider O'Shea and also Toth and Schick.
39. See tools of the Oldowan industry from Bed I at Olduvai Gorge (especially taken from J. Desmond Clark see p. 69 of *Prehistory of Africa*. Flakes and utilized notches were like knives (i.e. utensils) used to cut as we eat.
40. Reader, p. 188.
41. Reader p. 169 who cites Leakey, M. D. (1979) and Reader on p. 173 also makes use of M.D. Leakey's diagram.

Chapter Twelve

Typologies and Black Prehumanity

CATEGORIES AD NASEUM

Who has the greatest interest in deciding what labels will be assigned to newly discovered fossil remains? A skull (or anatomical vestige) is found and paleontologists immediately take it to mean that it will be identified one way or another; inevitably and logically it must belong to one species or it helps to devise a new entity. Thinkers like Dart contended for a new creation of human ancestry and they competed against others with differing perspectives on African-derived archaeological catches that involve definitions concerning prehumanity. Donald Johanson and Mary Leakey battled the big question of which personally discovered African species is the true descendant, the true grandmother of them all, i.e., Abraham's biblical wife, Sarah herself, mother of endless generations; this competiveness for prehuman singularity encompasses the fossil remains from Afar or the other one from the Laetoli as first prehuman. This researching mêlée in the late 1970's and early 1980's minimally considered the extreme sexual dimorphism analyzed between the various finds from both locations.

Perceived multiple forms as they accrue implicate contending credibilities. Direct presentations generate intellectual movements that date back to the twentieth century. Scientific analyses and fashioned imagined entities have been allocated from African spaces and all of which comprise notions of prehumanity and extend a racialized and genderized African black existentialism. Moreover, both racialized and genderized constructs can be perceived. Scientific studies about the past present somatic and devised sexualities. Deciding what to observe and how we assign skeletons in this scientific present really determines a utilitarian past and thus the past is generated. The culture of scientism stages and fixates bones and thus models or formulates genders incognizant of nature's plasticity and mutability.[1] Varying categorized and subcategorized forms are hard to blend. The *Homo* and *Australopithecus* forms are intentionally consigned not to be sold but to be used for reconstructive purposes of the past. Of course, this leads to demarcate and reconstitute ultimately within a binary construction and yet *Homo* and australopithecine inventions are found within a remote geographic and stratigraphic region.

Afar is 2,000 kilometers (1,242.74 miles) away from Laetoli. Mary Leakey had thought that the Afar and Laetoli finds represented two different species. Donald Johanson and Tim White believed them to be one and the same. Quantitatively one could go onwards *ad infinitum* to assert that various specimens are as different as they seem because of, for example, the dimensions of a prognathic face, or because of differing nuchal planes, or short or medium ilia, with small or medium sciatic notches, varying pelvic dimensions, encephalizational rates, an ascending mandibular, an increasing ramus, etc. etc. etc. Nevertheless, it seems that through seriation, clines and clusters of discoveries accrue and only complement the great ambiguity that still presently exists. The nature of science then is to create utilitarian divides precipitated by notions that offer a ruse of precision.

Again, Afar and Laetoli are about 2,000 kilometers (1,242.74 miles) away from each other and Mary Leakey had always thought that they each maintained two very differing hominid forms. Johanson who worked at the Afar site believed that their new form, *A. afarensis*, was the same. They even went on to name their type specimen after a Laetolian australopithecine. They used an adult mandible from Laetoli with a maximum age of 3.7 m. y. a., which meant *Homo* dates as early as australopithecines in the prehuman-to-human prearrangement despite any anatomical ambiguities.

Contemporary thoughts on dimorphism do not dissuade singularities within the prehuman-to-human journey. One impression about prehuman-to-human movement has undoubtedly remained proof positive and that is that the hominids from Afar and Laetoli, and for that matter East Turkana, had proven that hominids were bipedal and walked somewhat erect before encephalizational increases. The Pliocene footprints found at the Laetoli Bed at Laetoli located in Northern Tanzania caused quite a sensation from 1977 through 1979 when they were first discovered. It is believed that from the Laetoli footprints and pelvic remains of Hadar that australopithecines were in some form of way bipedalistic.[2] And yet, some have argued that archaeological work neglects or overlooks other skeletal requisite changes for straight upright walking and argue that they have to be thoroughly evaluated. The analyzed australopithecines were considered preadaptive for bipedal walking and were theoretically considered halfway to the evolutionarily changed position of the present day human. Their skeletal structure shows that they were very much capable of tree climbing as well. Archaeology also considered the

5 m. y. a. climatic impact and those climatic alterations which precipitated the advancing development of gracile australopithecines. Some have presented the rationalistic assumption that change in climate necessitated bipedalism which may have been a way for australopithecines' continued survival.

There are some who would believe climatic changes to savannah and drier treeless open spaced environments led the way to the inevitable wandering australopithecines. Gracile, *robustus* and *Homo habilis* were all devised by these climatic changes and *robustus* who had been too behemoth for the changes had a difficult time adjusting to less and less treeless environments, there were less and less hard crushing fruits and nuts that fell from the less and less self-replicating trees because there had been less and less high level pluvial activity. Natural alterations caused by the earth's self-regulatory system (or rather patterned system) that perhaps caused lakes to evaporate. These geo-activated changes would have been nothing less than cyclic catastrophisms to hominids at respective time periods.[3] Less specialized australopithecines went on to adapt to cultural developments that would have brought forth better and better survival maneuverings. Prehuman typologies or divisions help in designing this alterprehumanity which can also be interpreted as a form of scientific resistance to human holism and or human unity. The divides serve to create imaginary segregated demarcations.

And in a ruse of specificity there is this belief of liberating objectivity and the dominant archaeological endeavor identifies territories and maintains a power relationship. This regulating liaison between paleoanthropologist and prehuman archaeological treasures includes a domineering force that contains controlled entities and creates serviceable origins. Creating alternative forms i.e., prehumans that are defined geographically and even culturally, Afar, Laetoli, Oldowan, Tuang, Zinj, austrolo-types, homo-types etc. etc. etc. all of which allude to a propensity for advancement i.e., as we get closer and closer to the insurmountable sapiens-type humanity remains in flux. Inherently, the colonialism of scientism manifests itself in this re-creation of an African and functional black past. Also, references to climatic contingent effects (i.e. the interaction between prehumanity and geoactivities of earth) are logically juxtaposed to and help justify prehuman dispersals and add to the *explananda* of derivatives and deviations.[4]

THE "MAN" AND (HIS) HEOPREHI(STORY)

Within the identified australopithecine arrangement, the connected hominids, particularly *afarensis*, became not only just large forms of apes, but also ancestors of humanity. Various australopithecines are interconnected: *africanus*, *robustus*, *rudolfo*, *boisei*, *afarensis*, etc. and with *Homo*: *habilis*, *erectus*, archaic *sapiens*, modern *sapiens* we have some further connectivity.

The large-brained *Homo habilis*, with its spatial level of 1470 cc, triumphed and extended toward the inexorable and endowed modern human. Disembodying these various forms and concepts interpreted from archaeological discoveries could be considered blasphemous, but one must note that specimens, i.e., remains, have been somewhat maintained tightly as if they were appropriated and claimed property and considered umbilically a derived resource (some of the critical remains have been extracted from African land and thus should be read as an African resource) and such displacement seems to fit the traditional exploitative pattern when Europeans depleted African resources for economic gain and continue to do so. The anatomical and artefactual prehuman remnants are appropriated and just like gold nuggets they have value even if they are located and maintained by African governments in African vaults.

Robert Gordon Latham (a nineteenth century ethnologist and philologist) in a book titled *Man and His Migrations* presented three great problems that complicated nineteenth century studies on ethnology and prehistory: (1) the unity or non-unity of human species, (2) its antiquity and (3) its geographical origin.[5] All three issues presented by Latham are very important issues that need to be well understood in order to deconstruct the paradigmatic scientism about prehistory and the idea of a black prehumanity. Beginning with the first Lathamian concept of unity and/or disunity, some African prehistoric scholars strictly focus on an abysmal realm of disunity among the human species. Researchers of the prehuman past fine-tune their labelization techniques *ad infinitum* and continue to differentiate to an unrecognizable and irresolvable complexity.

African prehistoric scholarship reviews and sorts ossified shades of whiteness and such interpretives contain what is black and what is not white and what is not white is not tan and what is not tan is not brown and so on. Skeletal meanings unfortunately include racial semiotics and are also read and racialized from shapes, curvatures, and forms. Anatomical objects must be identified and ultimately its metageography alludes to social delineation. Defining prehumanity does not include nonlabelization of remnants; the study of bones neglects the plausibility of multiple connectives because every piece dug from the earth must inevitably have its scripted body. It was J. Desmond Clark who began to complain about archaeological work done before WW II where he noticed that site assemblages particularly in the prehistoric African horizons could not be compared because the work done before the Second World War had been too generalistic and waste products of tools were discarded.[6] The generalities were not specific enough and either required precise divisions or must recognize the interconnections within and among assemblages. Interconnections can include the process of comparability, which would mean appraisals about connectors to various site assemblages. Two tools that look the same and work the same even if 2, 000 km away from each other between Afar and Laetoli for example can be considered a connective.

With the second Lathamian thought, i.e. its antiquity and its scheme of timeframes, we are interminably in search of the antiquity of "man." Archaeology makes the "original man" and such relative terms move backwards to discover the oldest hypothetical Adam otherwise considered "the antique man." Scientism dissects prehistory (or ethnology as Latham's profession would have been known—Gamble and others modify it) vis-à-vis the study of primordial forms in the guise of an envisioned metonymy of humanity. Archaeology prehistoricizes further and further back to the point of creating the ever-so-moving-forward semi-pithecine ("ape") form. The antiquity of our species adds information to scientism and recognizably archaeology. It is through the field of anthropology, "study of man," and it is through paleoanthropology, i.e., the "study of man of the past" that now include the obstinate geneticist (more specifically and more redundantly the "genetico-archaeo-ontologist"). Intellectually, various *explanada* implicate the palaeontologist and the paleobiologist in the (re)discovery of that originating and primary ancient entity. The imageries devolve into a deeper and deeper past with its endless accruement of re-creative synecdoches of "man" long past and of an extant (and yet still searchable and enigmatic "man") which, in a capacious sense, the process of scientism radiates human sensibilities about the past.

Latham's last concern is a critical one for eco-geographically determined habitats are suppositional and prehistorical in a way that also reflects archaeology's empowerment over the past. Nevertheless, the locality of most hominids, in the case of australopithecines, is solely restricted to Africa. Early pithecines are limited topographically and are specified within time-frames in an African past. Climate and moistures are forces that designate finds even. Other parts of the world outside of Africa have not been so preserving. The prehistoric appearance of australopithecines dominates the varied hominid species selections and originates solely in Africa. Unfortunately, australopithecines have been used to explain away Africa's worldly presence and also used to connote primitivism and inferiority. Thus, Madison Grant and Lothrop Stoddard's beliefs in a particular typology's human retrograding propensity away from "advanced" existence were useful in the early twentieth century. Africa-first entities were used to build on prior race thinking and geoprehistories plague human parity. Despite an African worldly presence, African prehistory and its juxtaposition to "advanced" humanity only relegates African human development to the prehuman status and are interpreted as existing solely at one point in time and theoretically consigned to stagnancy.

AFRICANIC CENTRI(CITIES)

Oldowan culture as a geographic representative had existed somewhere in the chronicled vicinity of 1.8 m. y. a. and later. Australopithecines began during a quantified time in the past. Again, as mentioned above, the KBS Tuff incident initially gave australopithecines an earlier date, as early as 2.6 m. y. a. Some paleontologists expound modern human linkage with sequential derivation from quasi-proto-human forms (i.e. australopithecines) and they note that they culturally and somewhat quite progressively existed in no other region than an African one.

Embellishments about forms and their meanings are not the issue, but instead the one-dimensional and one-directional presumption of human movement is. Assessments about the primitive-to-modern or prehuman-to-human peculiarities disallow interconnectivity and offer a limited spatial breath that envisions itemized anatomical scriptures. Australopithecines, *habiles*, and *erecti* forms have been considered end-forms functionally and are trumped by other forms with grander encephalizational rates for example. Teleologically, humanity is conceived as moving and advancing toward the present. Views of movement are in sync with antebellum sentiments about a peculiar American system. Prehuman and primitive types are deemed obsolete and endowed with a long awaited extinction. Archaeological reconstructions then implicate imaginary prehuman African types and although Africa premieres in global human prehistories it seems that Africans are inevitably bound by extinct spaces. The centrality of Africa in (pre)histories becomes valorized only up to a fixed point in the past and unescapably such defined junctures precipitate a dehumanized slate that extends to contemporary human affairs. Its legacy (i.e. its prehuman and African) is deliberated by scientism and exposes a molded travelled path from the past that is singular and carries an antiquated identity.

Moreover, scientism explains away Africa-centrality highlighting the ecological and environmental and Africa's stratigraphic preservatives that subjugate Asian, European, and even American *in situ* finds. African exclusivity and provenances have been construed as antithetical to global multiplicity and human parity. The out-of-Africa model serves to reaffirm prehuman-to-human transitional voyages from the past to the advanced hierarchical Western type. Nevertheless, outside African regions with similar preservation environments compete with rich finds that are used to back the concept of motion and advancement. In the end, australopithecines are African and these African australopithecines lived a cultural life no matter how rudimentary it may have once seemed.

African Australopithecines persisted whether in home bases beside lakes or rivers and/or within caves since some of the caves were near rivers and lakes. Johanson and others portrayed and characterized apes living like humans and walking in pastures as seen in a former *Time* magazine issue. Australopithecine types of *africanus* and *afarensis* were directly linked to Homo. They are also predominantly held as a separated grouping especially after the discovery at the Nachukui Formation in the Omo region in the Plio-Pleistocene sediment of a hyper-robust australopithecine. The discovered specimen was KNM-WT 17000 (unfortunately due to its bone coloration otherwise known as the "Black Skull," i.e. a *robustus* form that was considered an outsider and due to its identification one that also reflects a scientific and social construction).

Africanus was linked with robust but at some later point in time *robustus*, it is believed, was led out to die. Again morphological identification of traits have somewhat confused matters with the various multiple varieties of alleged taxa forms. It is assumed given the extensively slow macroevolutinary process that most comparative skeletal details found cannot be a valid predictor of phylogenetic passages of convergence, in other words we will probably never find sufficient detail similarities along the variant hominids to point out perceptive dotted increments on a connecting and straight "ascending" line that would be evolutionarily revealing and display directive links to the supposed wonderful world of Indo-European advancement.

The term "missing link" was a sensationalistic word used for many years throughout a postDarwinian age. There are enough "missing links" in the archaeological record to be claimed by an army of paleoanthropologists, paleontologists, paleobiologists, paleogeneticists etc. etc. etc. for an eternity. During the sixties and seventies the eye catching term had become "oldest man" which presented an image of the "first man" of humanity which was later subsequently prevailed by the "first man" on earth and then onto the "first man" on the moon and then the "first man" found under a microscope. There are more creative ways of reinventing and rediscovering humanity from a pre-ordained humanity on this planet to better or rather to find even greater insight into our existence or how we project how humanity came to be. The stories never cease and we must come to understand that we can forever create links with other forms of life, but what we must really do is make better present living links with ourselves and the endless forms of subspecies that we have come to create.

Origins are plentiful and yet according to Frank Hole, the origin of the *Homo sapiens* occurs in a bottleneck fashion in various locations that subsequently come to several appearances of a multitude of archaic people occurring throughout.[7] Again, we have not yet discovered later versions of pithecines outside of Africa. Bipedal australopithecine types are mostly African and australopithecines did live contemporaneously with African *Homo habilis* and as of yet only *Homo habilis* has been deemed the one who began to lead into further high level development of "wise" humanity.

The term *Homo habilis* was assigned by a group of paleontologists, John Napier, Louis Leakey, and Phillip Tobias. He was named *Homo habilis* because it meant "man having the ability to manipulate tools" and stone tools have been found which were linked to habilines from the bottom of Bed I into the lower part of Bed II.[8] *H. habilis* was a composite made of varying yet somewhat similar looking pithecines found in one particular region of Africa and it had always remained somewhat questionable as to its exact gestalt.[9] They are referred to as ancestors which are believed to be human. And so this newly devised subspecies of hominid was assigned the *Homo* term back in the mid 1960's. This species was a particular favorite of Louis Leakey. In the general consensus of beliefs we are also told that before the arrival of *Homo sapiens* we have *Homo habilis* who from the neck down differs little from that of Australopithecus. The only difference is that the cranium is somewhat larger in *habilis*. A larger brain would certainly explain the rise to use stone tools by this novel handy cerebral group one would think. We also do find tools beside australopethecines as well.

We do know that East African *H. habilis* did use tools as well.[10] Also we must believe that the toolmaker must think abstractly in order to make the product that will accomplish the task needed.[11] What becomes quite problematic is how did *H. habilis* scavenge or hunt. Again, archaeological studies can only speculated as to what early hominids have done. Archaeologically there are many challenging uncertainties such as marks made on bones found which animal teeth, U-shaped grooves or hominid tools, V-shaped grooves, could have made. Determining that the animal was dead or alive before being butchered is difficult to assess again archaeologically. Tools are found but precisely how were they used remains somewhat speculative. Binford argued that "early hominids performed archaeologically invisible activities, we could learn a great deal from tools about adaption but we just don't have enough in early years."[12] If *H. habilis* was a forager or hunter, then he must have found his way out of Africa while he scavenged and hunted discovering ever so often more varying horizons and peering further out into newly reformed habitable lands. Yet he does not find his way out of one continent because we do not find any *H. habilis* outside of Africa. at the times of his existence. Just as all the austrolopithecines so too are all the *Homo habilis* species discovered as of yet found solely in Africa.[13]

THE ERECTINE FORM: BRICOLÁGE AND DIFFERÁNCE

As time progresses in a steady continuum since the appearance of hominids, we come to *H. erectus* a species that at one time had also existed in three continents. *H. erectus* is widely geographically located throughout various regions, and this assertion had been ideal for a strong *a priori* stance that modern human evolutionary development did not exist solely in one particular place, such as an "African homeland hypothesis" has rendered, but instead adaptative developmental processes are believed to have occurred at several different sites throughout three continents where some of these later pithecines have already been discovered out of Africa. One could say that *Homo erectus* remained quite distinct yet similar in and out of Africa, as they further anthropo-metamorphosized. They reason that since various early *H. erecti* have been located outside of Africa, then varying changes must have also occurred in nonAfrican localities as well. Another complication of processual change is that some pithecines have existed contemporaneously with what has been construed as earlier forms.

Also, "Zhoukoudian man" had been found around the same time, located in northeastern China, near Beijing at a mining installation called Zhoukoudian. If we consider the Java find along with forty other finds in China referred to as *Sinanthropus*, *Homo erectus*. Both "Zhokoudian man" and *Sinathropus* are later dated specimens of Hominines targeting primarily *H. erectus*. However, a *H. erectus* has not been found anywhere in Europe.[14] According to Howells the kinds of *Homo* found in the Far East can be broken down into various regions and it seems that after *erectus* the fossil record becomes quite poor and this of course leads him to assert that it had been populated late.[15]

A counterargument that some could use would be that the oldest version of *Homo erectus* ever found to date and the most completed specimen would have to be the "Turkana boy" (KNM, WT 15000), a twelve year old boy which had been discovered in July 1984 by the Leakey Team at a volcanic deposit dated 1.65 m. y. a. (The fossil remains are also to be equally dated). The volcanic deposit is located on the east shore of lake Turkana in Kenya.[16] One could further agree that similar and older traditions of the Acheulian industry (named after a place in France call St. Acheul where the type of tools [handaxes, etc.] were first identified) can be found in Africa.[17] We can note that outside Africa and Asia there are few hominid finds and that there are no hominid remains that date to before the Middle Pleistocene anywhere in Europe.[18] The oldest site in Europe would be Soleilhac in France where artifacts and faunal remains (a site without any hominid finds) has been dated to 800,000 years ago.[19] It has clearly been proven that *Homo erectus* was an ingenuitive hominid because the type was capable of expanding out into Asia and Europe and the type had been a species that remains in existence for over one million years.[20] And throughout this time all the *erecti* found throughout have remained quite unchanged; there are no major leaps in change.[21]

But how again did we get to *H. erectus* at those "out of African" sites? Did it take three million years to depart Africa? One could certainly consider this one of the earliest African diaspora with a string of more to follow. If we read the present story review a supposed time when our hominid ancestors first placed their feet on the ground and moved about and then transitioned from 4 million years ago (from anthropoids) onto chimpanzees who transformed to bipedal apes and then became walking and contemplative and naked human beings ultimately arriving at "advancement," we nonetheless understand that the process of development of the human species can be still considered furtive. Why was Africa the place for continual sequential change and no other places where early various prehistoric pithecines have been discovered contemporaneously existing in differing forms? Why was change limited to one specific area for a time until we come to a catacalysmic boom and *voila* multiple locational existences occur outside of Africa?

The legendary Richard Leakey, son of the venturous Louis Leakey, believed that humanity did not become conscious, compassionate, moral and creative when prehumanity transpired into *Homo sapiens*, but a long time before when she or he is identified as *Homo erectus*. According to Leakey "[a]bout a million years ago, populations of *Homo erectus* began to move out of Africa and into various regions of the old World, taking the Acheulean technology with them."[22] Leakey saw *Homo erectus* as foraging species that never resided at the same location for more than several days.[23]

> *Homo erectus* stands at a pivotal point in human evolutionary history; in a very real way it is the harbinger of humanity. Everything earlier than *Homo erectus* was more apelike (except the short-lived, somewhat enigmatic *Homo habilis*). Everything after *Homo erectus* was distinctly humanlike, in behavior as well as form. The beginnings of a hunting-and-gathering way of life came with Homo erectus, stone tools for the first time gave the impression of standardization, the imposition of a metal template, ore was harnessed for the first time, for the first time hominids expanded beyond the African continent. And surely the rudiments of language—perhaps even consciousness—were produced in a dramatically expanding brain.[24]

Thus, *Homo erectus*, for this scholar and many others reading the past, becomes the defining line between ape and modern humanity, i.e. this becomes the standard presented trajectory to wise Indo-European "man." We are also informed that this transformation occurred 1.6 million years ago. What this great paleoanthropologist asserts was also asserted by his mother, Mary Leakey, who gently claimed on a warm spring evening that the beginnings of humanity could not have evolved anywhere else other than Eastern Africa.[25] What is inferred by both Leakeys is that *Homo erectus* was the great traveler that went from Africa out into Asia and then on into Europe.

It can be believed that because of hominid spreads we have the results of genetic isolated variance portrayed in the fossil record. We know that quadrapedal early pithecines are already found in sites outside of Africa early on in our prehistory. But what do we make of the later varieties of bipedalistic *Homo* versions which were believed to have been foragers and even scavengers and thus because of their wanderings and subsistence patterns it is also believed that they had to have traveled and dispersed in very far out reaches distant from Africa? One would think that because of this developmental fashion of eating migrational movements occurred and that inclusively *Homo sapiens sapiens* derivatives have multiple genetically and newly created birthplaces dating to the existence of *Homo erectus*.[26] According to Haviland modern *Homo sapiens* birthplace was *in situ* in several coexisting populations between 100 - 40,000 years ago.[27] A Michigan school of thought propounded by Wolpoff argued that human evolution was primarily influenced by the occurrence of one single human species that "internally divided into races." Wolpoff presented the idea that

> [h]uman populations developed a network of interconnections. Behavioral and genetic information was interchanged by mate exchanges and population movements. Gradients along these interconnections encouraged local adaptations. These and other sources of population variation that depended on population histories developed, and stable adaptive complexes of interrelated features evolved in different regions. But, at the same time, evolutionary changes across the species occurred as advantageous features appeared and dispersed because of the success they imparted. These changes took on different forms in different places because of the differing histories of populations reflected in their gene pools, and the consequences of population placements in terms of habitat and their relations to other populations. Some evolutionary changes happened everywhere, because of these processes and because of common aspects of selection created by the extra information exchanges allowed by the evolving cultural and communications systems. Consequently, throughout the past 2 million years humans have been a single widespread polytypic species, with multiple, constantly evolving, interlinked populations, continually dividing and merging. Because of these internal division and processes that maintain them, this species has been able to encompass and maintain adaptive variations across its range without requiring the isolation of gene pools.[28]

Wolpoff defines the multiregional model and one key element about this theory that needs to be emphasized in this Wolpoffian story on origins is "interconnections." According to Wolpoff there is no "isolation of gene pools." The key element that Wolpoff does not mention enough is Africa remained connected. The notion of human development throughout the Old World involves spreads, or what one could refer to as Diasporas, that also involved an African presence. Wolpoff understands that with spreads there must be connectedness, a very important criterion for human persistence even early on and continuing forward to what can be erroneously construed as Indo-European advancement. And so, humanity and for the sake of this argument has always remained "interlinked," each grouping cannot remain entirely autonomous.

This Wolpoffian idea could be considered a diffusionist idea about the development of humanity. And like the contention about the development of culture so too do we find contentions about origins and humanity. Scientism and the quest for defining the story of humanity and how it came to be is in the same realm of capturing the first idea. Ideas then are first created and then given to (or stolen by) somebody else rather than developing independently in different times and places. Ideas then have a value and if the notion is that these values are interconnected then there is the belief that there was unity that includes prehumanity, i.e. an African prehumanity. This alternative analysis emphasizes multiplicity and does not imply anything about the veracity of scientific claims because this deconstruction is interested in the phenomena of ideas presented about a black past its so-called prehumanity. Books were certainly useful in reconstructing thought patterns about ancestry. The archaeological record is helpful in examining prehumanity whether the prehuman to human trajectory is considered mythical and/or allegorical. Hi(stories) *de homine* are part of the enterprise of a post-colonial system that continues to conquer with notions of movement and its central *novus* meaning. Every research and perceptions about prehumanity maintains that its "objectivity" plays a central role in the story they present. And yet, to decenter the prehuman and African in order to unveil parity is the problem of the twenty-first century quest for origins *de homine*.

NOTES

1. See Anne Fausto-Sterling *Sexing the Body: Gender Politics and the construction of sexuality* Basic books (2000) and also see *Sign 30* no. 2 (2005) p. 1491–1527.
2. Berge, pp. 259–273.
3. Potts, p. 47–48. See his stratigraphic analysis of Olorgasailie in Kenya.
4. See Potts again.
5. See Lantham (1851) p. 49 which is cited in Gamble (1993) p. 40.
6. Clark, p. 38.
7. Frank Hole's lecture on World Prehistory on Jan. 26, 1993 at Yale University. Mithen, because of a confirmed lack of extensive genetic diversity, presents a scenerio of six breeding individuals for every seventy year period and approximates about 50 to 500 for about 200 years within which a boom occurs. Mithen also cites Jones et al. (1992) and Jones and Rouhani (1986).
8. Clark, p. 59 and Leakey, Tobias, & Napier, p. 7–9.
9. Tattersall p. 116 states that *habilis*' split from austrolopithecines was questionable and that its form is quite variable.
10. Haviland p. 169 and182, Johansen p. 96, and Leakey (1994) p. 123 and who also states that handaxes were not used until *erectus* and not *habilis* p. 40. What makes this a critical tool is that they are used for chopping meats and bones from carcasses instead of biting and tearing.
11. Ibid., p. 179.
12. Binford p. 302.
13. Feder p. 244.
14. Howells p. 141.
15. P. 195.
16. Feder, p. 240–41 who cites Leakey and Walker (1985).

17. Ibid., p. 253.
18. Ibid., p. 249 Feder (first edition) p. 179 who cites Cook *et al.*
19. Feder (third edition), p. 249 and Feder (first edition) p.180 where he cites Weaver, Feder remains consistent throughout editions.
20. Feder, p. 259.
21. Ibid., p. 260 and 261 and Feder (first edition) p. 191 where he cites also Rightmire, Cronin et al., Wolpoff(1980), Binford and Chuan p. 429, and Leigh.
22. (1977) p. 226.
23. Ibid., p. 189.
24. Ibid., p. 46–47.
25. Mary Leakey asserted an African homeland hypothesis in a graceful presentation on April 22, 1993 at Davenport College, Yale University.
26. See Cavalli-Sforza on migration.
27. P. 242.
28. P. 32 [Italic as used by Wolpoff (1997)]. Also, note that the last line in this Wolpoff quote is the opposite of what George Lauder stated and what Wolpoff is counterarguing.

Conclusion

Cheikh Anta Diop is considered to be one of the greatest scholars to come out of the African world in the twentieth century. He was born in Diourbel, Senegal in 1923 and had an untimely death in 1986. He has been described as being the founder of a "new concept" of African history. *African Origins of Civilization*, is a one-volume translation of the major sections of two other books titled *Nations negres et Culture* and *Anteriorite des civilizations negres*. Both of these works have challenged and changed the directions of attitudes about the place of the African peoples in world history. His works initially date back to the 1950s which were translated into English in 1974. His ideas have been the prime catalyst for a total reconsideration of the role that African people have played in history and their impact on the development of early civilizations. Diopian strengths, but also its prophetic visions about what is at stake when dealing with the prehuman to human legacy includes African ubiquity.

Some prehistorians and archaeologists agree that the great evolution of humanity first occurs in the African continent; however, others have differing opinions. There has always been this denial to not believe in the Africanness of a primordial being just as there has been this varying tone and strong adversity to the belief of an African origin of civilization and human culture. African origins of anything, culture, prehumanity and also humanity is a contentious topic because it reflects present social hierarchical standing about what region developed first and paved the way for "advanced" humanity and no matter how objective a origins stance or position may portend it still nonetheless reflects present human association. Cheikh Anta Diop, a native of Senegal and an African scholar trained initially in physics and then later switching to anthropology obtained his *Docteur es Lettres* from the University of Paris. He obtained his degree with some resistance because he had professed very early on in his academic training the very controversial theory that Egypt was a black African civilization and that the birthplace of humanity was black Africa. He believed not only that "Grimaldi Man" who was found in Italy is considered to be African, but also that archaic *Homo sapiens* ought to be construed as black and thus quintessentially African. He decisively argued that

> [i]n the Upper Paleolithic, the archaic *Homo sapiens* either disappeared or else evolved into the Grimaldi man, for only the latter has been found, without any parallel branch of *Homo sapiens* until the belated appearance of the Cro-Magnon and Chancelade races.[1]

The Diopian *argumentum* concerning the human past situates an African in European geographical space. The idea of African dispersals or African diffusion into the European realm advances against the very origins of Indo-Europeaness and it makes a case for human global fluidity which is linked to the African. Diop's assessment has been considered diatribe because it opposed scientism's crucial tradition directly. In another segment Diop continued with the following:

> All the human types found in Kenya from the Paleolithic to the end of the Neolithic, are perfectly distinguishable as Negroes. Dr. Leakey who has studies nearly all of them, knows this. He knows that all the skeletons that have fallen into his hands have Negritic proportions in the full sense of the word. He also is aware that the observations by Boule and Vallois on the "floor of the nasal fossae" is applicable to all the skulls that he has studied. One can understand why anthropologists are silent on these determining points. On the contrary, they readily expand on cranial measurements, for in this domain, except in extreme cases, it is harder to distinguish a Negro from a White. They admit, for example, that from the Paleolithic to our day Kenya, East Africa, and the Upper Nile have been inhabited by the same population which has remained anthropologically unchanged.[2]

Diop countered anthropological and archaeological researchers that he believed conspired and have been somewhat concertedly biased in their analyses of prehistoric evolutionary humanity. Diopian discernments of the past offered an African derivation that located African membership and recognition in human origins because African entities were customarily relegated to secondary and tertiary levels in the human trajectory to "progress." Reviewers of the past have fixated or negated African participation in several fronts and made African forms diminutive as they continued to catalogue forms that carry meanings about the prehuman-to-human sequence. Diop further pointed out that

> [w]henever they discuss the late appearance of the 'true Negro,' we must remember that this is because they do not consider him as such, for he has been there since the beginning of time, since the Paleolithic. All the skull specimens considered non-Negroid, following the measurements of Leakey and other anthropologists, are really those of his archaeological forbearers from whom he does not differ morphologically. Dr. Leakey and all the anthropologist will confirm this.[3]

Diop maintained that anthropologists were inventors who distorted African history by not including the truthful presence of "Negroids', Hamites, semi-Hamites, Nilo-Hamites, Ethiopians, Sabaeans, and thus even Caucasoids"[4]

Diop's formation of African types represents not only something more than scientific anthropologists would commonly think but also a term that is quite antiguous to a well-established European centered scientific belief system. Diop disputed prior assessments while working through archaeological and prehistorian ideas and their reconstruction of humanity's past. He perhaps can be considered inherently a precursor and an extension of the American Black Power movement that defied scientific social injustices. Diop's consciousness revealed a skewed and devised human past. He connected his origin of human species with his origin of human civilization and adds that

> [t]he Negro has been there from the beginning; for millennia he was the only one in existence. Nevertheless, on the threshold of the historical epoch, the "scholar" turns his back on him raises questions about his genesis, and even speculates "objectively" about his tardy appearance.[5]

Diop was quite concern about interpretations of the prehuman past and has written extensively on where they may have faltered in their analyses back in the 1950s. His work moved from the so-called Paleolithic fabrications to notions of an out of Africa birth place for civilization.

Cheikh Anta Diop professed a very controversial theory all throughout his life and he had always been in agreement with the Leakeys. Diop implemented a corrective model and had turned to Hominine development and draped a racial color line upon the humanoid transformational process. Skulls became somewhat ethnicized and maintained skin color. The key archaeological finds in a Diopian arsenal are those in Swascombe and Fontechevade. One of the oldest European sites, located in the Charente region of France, at sites such as Fontechevade and La Chaise, which are believed to be around 200,000 years old. They were excavated back in the 1960s and 1970s by Andre Debenath and over eighty fossils were found there and even a skull with supposed Neandertalic features.[6]

There are older sites in Europe where finds have been found in 1992 in Atapuerca, Spain where three partial skulls claimed to date back to 300.000

years that supposedly portray "glimpses of the Neanderthal's imperialistic predecessor," an intermediate of *Homo erectus* and Neanderthal.[7] Diop believed that "Gramaldi Man" was African and that the existence of archaic *Homo sapiens*, Swascombe "Man" and Fontechevade "Man" in particular, are as early as the Lower Paleolithic. He claimed the following:

> In the Upper Paleolithic, the archaic Homo sapiens either disappeared or else evolved into the Grimaldi man, for only the latter has been found, without any parallel branch of Homo sapiens until the belated appearance of the Cro-Magnon and Chancelade races.[8]

Grimaldi "Man" came from the Mousterian sites and Diop insisted that there is no other variety of *H. Sapiens* that precedes "the Grimaldi Negroid" in Europe or in Asia.[9] Conservatively, it is believed that at some point in time mankind must have abandoned the African plains to seek havens in the many caves of Europe, Le Moustier being one of the first sites.[10] Diop makes this assertion as well and becomes indignant about the forgery of "Piltdown Man," a forgery that would have been a primary source for an alleged structure that would have given Europe an early prehistoric tradition and helped to support a European, separate, unique and ultimately "advanced" form. Diop continues with asserting that

> [a]ll the human types found in Kenya from the Paleolithic to the end of the Neolithic, are perfectly distinguishable as Negroes. Dr.[Louis] Leakey who has studied on nearly all of them, knows this. He knows that all the skeletons that have fallen into his hands have Negritic proportions in the full sense of the word. He also is aware that the observations by Boule and Vallois on the floor of the nasal *fossae* is applicable to all the skulls that he has studied. One can understand why anthropologists are silent on these determining points. On the contrary, they readily expand on cranial measurements, for in this domain, except in extreme cases, it is harder to distinguish a Negro from a White. They admit, for example, that from the Paleolithic to our day Kenya, East Africa, and the Upper Nile have been inhabited by the same population, which has remained anthropologically unchanged, with the Masai as one of the most authentic representative types.[11]

On this assertion of an East African origin Diop depends on a French scientist and a paleontologist, Boule and Vallois. This particular book by Diop (a translation of a combination of two French written books dating back to 1954 and 1967) on an African origin had been written before Louis Leakey's death in 1972. Louis Leakey also concurred along with his wife and son who continued to maintain an African origin long after Louis died. Despite the Leakeys' bearing on African origins, Diop saw an anthropological conspiracy among European scientists concerning the African remains and human origin. According to Wenke,

> [w]e know that the first million years or more of the history of our genus were spent in the Tropics of Africa and Asia, and we were probably all Africans until just a million years ago—late in our evolutionary story. Even if evidence for our ancestors' invasion of Asia before a million years ago is confirmed, we must still look to the grasslands and forests of Africa for proof about our origins.[12]

Diop had argued this same similar point all throughout his life. He believed Europeans as form and type appearing as Cro-Magnon "Man" around 20,000 years ago. According to Diop, "[Cro-Magnon Man] is probably the result of a mutation from the Grimaldi Negroid due to an existence of 20,000 years in an excessively cold climate of Europe at the end of the last glaciation."[13] The changes then are considered successive and this unfortunately lends itself to first race notions that still reflect movement from primitive to advancement. He went on further to state that

> [t]he first Homo sapiens who inhabited Europe was unquestionably a migrant Negroid who came from outside, about 40,000 years ago, as Rene Verneaux has demonstrated. The first "White", the Cro-Magnon Man, appeared in the same region 20,000 years later. Who was the ancestor of Cro-Magnon, if he did not derive from the Negroid through mutations? For neither the Cro-Magnon nor the Negroid descended from Neanderthal Man who preceded them and who lived 80,000 years ago, during the *Wurmian* period.[14]

One wonders if there is always movement and if in a time span of 20,000 years some subtle human changes occur. There are multiple theories concerning the color of skin and its development and it cannot be reviewed here.

One of the simplest traits used to present the conception of origins of "race" is skin color. It is commonly held that sunny Africa as with other parts of the world such as in India and New Guinea helped precipitate the development of blackish skins produced by melanin a naturalistic protective skin color coat against the sun's rays,. It seems that the further one moves north away from the Equator the paler the skin become as well as other things such as stoutness to maintain bodily warmth. There is no doubting that sun causes skin to darken. Dark skin protects against the burning caused by sun exposure.

What seems to trouble us in trying to maintain this theory of sun and dark skin and less sun and paler skin is that Natives (like the Inuit peoples from the artic regions of Greenland, Canada, and the United States) with dark skin dwelled in areas receiving relatively little sunlight. Take for example Tasmanians, or Native Americans whose skin has not changed to black skin and who dwelled in very sunny environments. According to Jared Diamond certain parts of the world that receive three and a half hours of sun daily include places like West Africa, South China and Scandinavia, and these places are inhabited by "some of the world's blackest, yellowiest, and palest peoples!"[15] The colors do not converge but remain multiple. Diamond continues to assert that the Solomon Islands have differing people that share the same climate, and yet there are jet-black people and lighter people who replace each other over short distances. Diamond presents a disproving picture when he states, "[e]vidently sunlight has not been the sole selective factor that influenced skin color."[16] Diamond goes on to present the counter argument that not enough time has passed to cause sufficient visible human change. He counter argues by stating that time is not an adequate factor. He gives the prime example that the "American Indians" (he means Native Americans) have reached the New World within only eleven thousand years and they still have not had visible change.

Jared Diamond's idea about climate theories and skin color contends that time is irrelevant because if you consider Scandinavians who have lived in Scandinavia a shorter period than those "American Indians" who lived in the Amazon the Scandinavians have not yet obtained the darkest skin complexion.[17] According to Diamond it seems that Scandinavians have spent half the time that the "American Indians" have spent in the Amazon. Diamond's pragmatic analysis on this very antagonistic topic only garnered just a few pages of his time in his work and he does not present his own solution to this problem other than to help discard all those logical assumptions on the origins of skin color. Blond hair and blue eyes in particular become also nonclimatic derived. Lastly, one can note that Jared Diamond's Tasmanians are not referred to as the darkest people in the region because color becomes irrelevant in his analysis but nevertheless he notes that they inevitably become an extinct group of people by the hands of colorizing and colonizing Europeans.[18]

Diop worked at preventing any future harmful archaeological creativity that only perpetuate unjust hierarchies and buttress purposeful nationalizations for one group to rule over another. The Piltdown incident was symptomatic of a scientific condition. Piltdown "man" had been a forgery discovered in 1912 by British geologist Charles Dawson.[19] Smith Woodward, Elliot Smith, Andrew Keith and others principally studied it, but Diop asserts that truth will always prevail, as science will always be apt to correct itself as Kenneth P. Oakley proved when he did a florine check and helped to prove its forgery.[20]

There are other critical scholars like Diop who worked at ameliorating the social present with the past. This enquiry specifically pertains to archaeological interpretations and certain conceptualizations about the Africanic. This work may seem antithetical to scientism, but its deconstructive intent was not to simplify and apply units of information but rather to isolate ideas about a constructed past and reveal some of its social implications. One aspect remains certain throughout this enquiry, and that is that scientific analyses involve multiple and variant readings. This theoretical enterprise concludes with yet another impression that is that a past then becomes heritage and is part of a formulated process. The past in the case of what has been termed the prehuman and Africanic supplies links to the present and thus can also be understood despite all its negative inferences as purposeful genealogy. To some its manifestation as a study of *genus* is considered sacred roots, i.e., in particular it is sacred to those who study the prehuman in the guise of self-proclaimed objectivity.

The constructed black past is sanctified in the sense that it entails the hallowed reaches of science, i.e. a knowledge-based realm that presumes acceptance due to its process. Scientism consequentially reflects human heritage, history, and the prehistory which all include beliefs about what is prehuman. It deems itself the valid seeker of truth and to that end it consigns most prior and other non-scientific readings as false or less precise. Ultimately, this deconstruction endeavor proffered no credulous allegiances to one school of thought nor did it urge ties to any one constricting disciplinary paradigm. In deconstructing the idea of the prehuman one discovers that past(s) seem(s) to remain tensile primarily in matters that include the Africanic.

NOTES

1. Diop (1967) p. 262.
2. Ibid., p. 273. It should be noted that these comments were written before Louis Leakey's death in 1972.
3. Ibid., p. 274.
4. Ibid., p. 274.
5. Ibid., p. 274.
6. Johanson, p. 260.
7. Ibid.
8. Diop (1967), p. 262.
9. Diop (1967) and also see Diop (1991) p. 15–16 on Gimaldi Negroid hypothesis.
10. Charles-Picard p. 147.
11. Diop (1967), p. 273.
12. p. 83.
13. Diop (1991), p. 15–16.
14. Ibid., p. 26 and here for this assertion Diop uses Hallam L. Dubois who uses Movius (a Harvard scholar) see Dubois p. 253.
15. p. 115.
16. Ibid.
17. p. 116.
18. Truganini and William Lanner. [see his illustrations].
19. Ibid., p. 29. Also, see Feder et al. p. 129 for this same kind of assertion on nationalism.
20. Diop (1991), p. 29.

Bibliography

Abend, H. (1929). "Peking Man Ranked as Oldest Human: Scientists Call Fossil Nearest Approach to Missing Link Yet Discovered." *The New York Times*. New York: III 8.

Adams, R. M. (1974). "Anthropoligical Perspectives on Ancient Trade." *Current Anthropology* 15: 239–258.

Allman, J. M. (1999). *Evolving Brains*. New York, Scientific American Library.

Altieri, C. (1990). *Canons and Consequences: Reflections on the Ethical Force of Imaginative Ideals*. Evanston, Ill., Northwestern University Press.

Angela, P. a. A. (1993). *The Extraordinary Story of Human Origins*. New York, Prometheus Books.

Ani, M. (1994). *Yurugu : an African-centered critique of European cultural thought and behavior*. Trenton, N. J., Africa World.

Aristotle, R. Waterfield, et al. (1996). *Physics*. Oxford; New York, Oxford University Press.

Baker, J. R. (1974). *Race*. New York, Oxford University Press.

Bakhtin, M. M., V. N. Voloshinov, et al. (1994). *The Bakhtin Reader: Selected Writings of Bakhtin*, Medvedev, and Voloshinov. London ; New York, E. Arnold.

Barrett, S. L. E. (1988 [1977]). *The Rastafarians: Sounds of Cultural Dissonance*. Boston, Beacon Press.

Benefit, B. R. a. M. L. M. (1995). "Miocene Hominoids and Hominid Origins." *Annual Review of Anthropology* 24: 237–256.

Boaz, N. T. (1997). *Eco Homo: How the Human Being Emerged from the Cataclysmic History of the Earth*. New York, Basic Books.

Bourdieu, P. and J. B. Thompson (1991). *Language and symbolic power*. Cambridge, Mass., Harvard University Press.

Brace, C. L. (1995). *The Stages of Human Evolution*. New York, Prentice Hall.

Brenton, S. L. C. L. (1999). *The Septuagint with Apocrypha: Greek and English*. London, Hendrickson Publishers.

Bynum, W. F., E.J. Browne, and R. Porter, Ed. (1981). *Dictionary of the History of Science*. Princeton, Princeton University Press.

Carmichael, S. (1968). *Power and Racism*. Radical perspectives on social problems; readings in critical sociology. F. Lindenfeld. New York, Macmillan: 240–248.

Cartmill, M. (1990). "Human uniqueness and theoretical content in paleoanthropology." *International Journal of Primatology* 11(3): 173–192.

Ciochon, R. L., Savage, D.E. Tint, T. and Maw, B. (1985). "New Discovery of Amphipithecus from the Eocene of Burma." *Science* 229: 756–759.

Clark, J. D. (1970). *The Prehistory of Africa*. London, Thames & Hudson.

Clark, W. L. G. (1978). *Antecedents of Man*. New York, Quadrangle Books.

Cole, J. B., Sheila S. Walker (1980). "Black Anthropology, Part 1." *The Black Scholar: Journal of Black Studies and Research* 11(7).

Cole, J. B., Sheila S. Walker (1980). "Black Anthropology, Part 2." *The Black Scholar: Journal of Black Studies and Research* 11(8).

Conroy, G. C. (1997). *Reconstructing Human Origins: a Modern Synthesis*. New York, W.W. Norton.

Considine, D. E., Ed. (1995). *Van Nostrand's Scientific Encyclopedia*. New York, Van Nostrand Reinhold.

Crovella, S., A. Brusco, A.O. Carbonara, S. Vellagan, M.P. Bugatti, L. Lamberti, M. Del Pero, Y. Rumpler and G. Ardito (1995). "Newly Evolved highly Repeated DNA Sequences of Tupaia glis (Tupaiidae, Scandentia)." *Human Evolution* 10(1): 45–52.

Culatta, E. (1995). "New Finds Rekindle Debate over Anthropoid Origins." *Science* 268: 1851.

Dawkins, R. (1995). *Out of Eden: A Darwin View of Life*. New York, Basic Books.

Dawkins, R. (1996 [1983]). *Universal Darwinism. But is it Science?: the Philosophical Question in the Creation/Evolution Controversy*. M. Ruse. New York, Prometheus Books.

Diamond, J. (1993). *The Third Chimpanzee: The Evolution and Future of the Human Animal*. New York, HarperCollins Publisher.

Diamond, J. M. (1997). *Guns, Germs, and Steel: the Fates of Human Societies*. New York, W. W. Norton & Company.

Dixon, D. (1990). *Man after Man: An Anthropology of the Future*. New York, St. Martin's Press.

Dobratz, B. A. a. S. L. S.-M. (1997). "White Power, White Pride:" *The White Separatist Movement in the United States*. New York, Twayne Publishers.

Drake, S. C. (1980). "Anthropology and the Black Experience." *The Black Scholar: Journal of Black Studies and Research* 11(7): 2–31.

Du Toit, A. L. (1937). *Our Wandering Continents; an Hypothesis of Continental Drifting*. Edinburgh, London, Oliver and Boyd.

Eagleton, M. (1996). *Feminist Literary Theory: a Reader*. Oxford, OX, UK ; Cambridge, Mass., Blackwell Publishers.

Eldridge, N. (1985). *Time Frames: The Rethinking of Darwinian Evolution and the Theory of Punctuated Equilibria*. New York, Simon and Schuster.

Ellison, R. (1989). *Invisible Man*. New York, Vantage Books Edition.

Everett-Heath, J. (2000). *Place Names of the World: Europe: Historical Context, Meanings And Changes*. Houndmills, Basingstoke, New York, NY, Macmillan Press; St. Martin's Press.

Falk, D. (1992). *Braindance*. New York, H. Holt.

Fausto-Sterling, Anne. *Sexing the Body: Gender Politics and the construction of sexuality*, New York, Basic Books (2000) and also see *Sign* 30 no. 2 (2005) p. 1491–1527.

Feagle, J. G. a. R. F. K. (1986). "The Fossil Record of Early Catarrhine Evolution." *Major Topics in Primate and Human Evolution*. B. Wood, L. Martin, and P. Andrews. Cambridge, Cambridge University Press.

Feagle, J. G. a. R. F. K. (1997). "Platyrrhines, Catarrhines, and the Fossil Record." *New World Primates: Ecology Evolution and Behavior*. W. G. Kinzey. New York, Aldine De Gruyter.

Feder, K. L., and M.A.Park (1997). *Human Antiquity: an Introduction to Physical Anthropology and Archaeology* (third edition). Mountain View: Mayfield Publishing Company. Mountain View, Mayfield Publishing Company.

Firmin, A. (2000). *The Equality of the Human Races* (*Positivist Anthropology*). New York and London, Garland Publishing, Inc.

Frolov, V. P. a. N., Igor D. (1998). *Black Hole Physics: Basic Concepts and New Developments*. Dordrecht/Boston/London, Kluwer Academic Publishers.

Gobineau, A., comte de, (1853–55). *Essai sur l'Inégalité des Races Humaines*. Paris.

Goold, G. P., Ed. (1996). *The Physics Book I-IV*. Cambridge, Harvard University Press.

Gould, S. J. a. R. C. L. (1979). "The spandrels of San Marco and the Panglossian Paradigm: a Critique of the Adaptationalist Programme." *Proceedings of the Royal Society*, London Series B 205: 581–598.

Gould, S. J. a. N. E. (1993). "Punctuated Equilibrium Comes of Age." *Nature* 366: 223–227.

Graves, J. L. (2001). *The Emperor's New Clothes: Biological Theories of Race at the Millennium*. New Brunswick, N.J.; London, Rutgers University Press.

Griffin, J. H. (1977). *Black like me*. Boston, Houghton Mifflin.

Gruesser, J. C. (2000). *Black on Black: Twentieth-century African American Writing about Africa*. Lexington, KY, University Press of Kentucky.

Grzimek, B. (1990). *Grzimek's Encyclopedia of Mammals*. New York, McGraw-Hill.

Gyekye, K. (1995). *An Essay on African Philosophical Thought: the Akan Conceptual Scheme*. Philadelphia, Temple University Press.

Gyekye, K. (1996). *African Cultural Values: an Introduction*. Philadelphia, PA, Sankofa Pub. Co.

Hage, G. (1998). *White Nation: Fantasies of White Supremacy in a Multicultural Society*. London, Routledge.

Haile-Selassie, Y. (2001). "Afar Ethiopia: human origins find 6 million years old bones, oldest so far." *Nature* 412: 178–181.

Hall, C. (1929). "Early Man Dug Up in Pacific Coast." *The New York Times*. New York: III 2.

Haviland, W. A. (1997). *Anthropology*. Philadelphia, Harcourt Brace College Publishers.

Hilliam, D. (1998). *Kings, Queens, Bones, and Bastards: Who's Who in the English Monarchy from Egbert to Elizabeth II*. Phoenix Mill, Thrupp, Stroud, Sutton.

Hodgen, M. T. (1964). *Early Anthropology in the Sixteenth and Seventeenth Centuries*. Philadelphia, University of Pennsylvania.

Hole, F. a. R. F. H. (1977). *Prehistoric Archaeology: A Brief Introduction*. New York, Holt, Renehart and Winston.

Hooton, E. A. (1931). *Up From the Apes*. New York, Macmillan.

Israel, W. (1998). "'Absurd and Ridiculous': The Collapse of Solidity. The black Hole: 25 Years After." J. Zanelli and C. Teitelboim. Singapore ; River Edge, N.J., *World Scientific*: 87–103.

Jacobsen, T. W. (1976). "17,000 years of Greek prehistory." *Scientific American* 234(6): 76–87.

Jones, J. S., R. Martin, and D. Pilbeam, Ed. (1992). *The Cambridge Encyclopedia of Human Evolution*. Cambridge, Cambridge University Press.

King, L. C. (1987). Gondwanaland. *The Encyclopedia of Structural Geology and Plate Tectonics*. C. K. Seyfert. New York, Van Nostrand Reinhold: 309–314.

Kurten, B. (1993). *Our Earliest Ancestors*. New York, Columbia University Press.

Lauder, G. V. (1996). "The argument from design." *Adaptation*. M. R. R. a. G. V. Lauder. California, Academic Press: 55–91.

Leakey, R. E. a. R. L. (1992). *Origins Reconsidered: In Search Of What Makes Us Human*. New York, Doubleday.

Lemonick, M. D. a. A. D. (2001). "The Dawn of Man." *Time Magazine*.

Lewin , R. (1997). *Patterns in Evolution: The New Molecular View*. New York, Scientific American Library.

Lovejoy, A. O. (1964). *The Great Chain of Being: A Study of the History of an Idea*. Cambridge, Harvard University Press.

Lowenthal, D. (1985). *The Past is a Foreign Country*. Cambridge [Cambridgeshire]; New York, Cambridge University Press.

Lyall, S. (1999). "A Country Unveils Its Gene Pool and Debate Flares." *New York Times*. New York.

Macvey, J. W. (1990). *Time Travel*. Chelsea, Mich., Scarborough House.

Marable, M. and L. Mullings (2000). *Let Nobody Turn us Around: Voices of Resistance, Reform, and Renewal: an African American Anthology*. Lanham, Md., Rowman & Littlefield.

Marino, L. (1996). "What can dolphins tell us about primate evolution?" *Evolutionary Anthropology* 5(3): 81–85.

Marks, J. (2000). "98% Alike?: What our Similarity to Apes tells us about our Understanding of Genetics." *The Chronicle of Higher Education*. XLVI: B7.

Martin, R. D. (1982). "Et tu, Tree Shrew?" *Natural History* 91(8): 26–33.

Maynard, R. (2001). "DNA Trace Puts Human Origins in Australia." *The Times*. London: 18.

Mbiti, J. S. (1990). *African religions & philosophy*. Oxford ; Portsmouth, N.H., Heinemann.
Megarry, T. (1995). *Society in Prehistory: The Origins of Human Culture*. New York, New York University Press.
Mithen, S. (1996). *Prehistory of the Mind: The Cognitive Origin of Art, Religion and Science*. London, Thames and Hudson.
Moses, W. J. (1996). *Classical Black Nationalism: from the American Revolution to Marcus Garvey*. New York, New York University Press.
Peterson, D. a. J. G. (1993). *Visions of Caliban on Chimpanzees and People*. Boston, Houghton Mifflin Company.
Potts, R. (1996). *Humanity's Descent: the Consequences of Ecological Instability*. New York, Avon Books.
Psellus, M. (1990). *Michaelis Pselli Commentarii in Physicen Aristotelis*. Stuttgart-Bad Cannstatt, Frommann-Holzboog.
Relethford, J. H. (1997). *The Human Species: An Introduction to Biological Anthropology*. California, Mayfield Publishing Company.
Renfrew, C. (1994). "World Linguistic diversity." *Scientific American* 270: 116–123.
Rich, P., V. Rich, T.H. Fenton, M. Adams Fenton, and C. Lane (1996). *The Fossil Book: A Record of Prehistoric Life*. New York, Dover Publication Inc.
Robinson, C. J. (1983). *Black Marxism: the Making of the Black radical tradition*. London, Zed.
Rose, M. (1983). "Miocene hominoid postcranial morphology: monkey-like, ape-like, neither, or both?" *New Interpretations of Ape and Human Ancestry*. a. R. S. C. R.L. Ciochon. New York, Plenum Press: 405–417 or 189–193.
Rosenberger, A. L. (1986). "Platyrrhines, catarrhines and the Anthropoid transition." *Major topics in Primate and Human Evolution*. L. M. Bernard Wood, and Peter Andrews. Cambridge, Cambridge University Press: 66–88.
Ruse, M., Ed. (1996). *But is it Science?: the Philosophical Question in the Creation/Evolution Controversy*. New York, Prometheus Books.
Rushton, J. P. (1997). *Race, Evolution, and Behavior: a Life History Perspective*. New Brunswick, N.J., Transaction Publishers.
Russell, B. (1963). *A History of Western Philosophy*. New York, Simon and Schuster.
Saussure, F. d. (1959). *Course in general linguistics*. New York, Philosophical Library.
Simons, E. L. a. D. R. P. (1965). "Preliminary Revision of the Drypithecinae (Pongidae, Anthropoidea)." *Folia Primatologica* 3(2–3): 81–152.
Simons, E. L. (1972). *Primate Evolution: An Introduction to Man's Place in Nature*. New York, Macmillan.
Simons, E. L. (1984). "Dawn ape of the Fayum, Tom, Dick, Harry, and Grant: the Faces are Familiar." *Natural History* 93(5): 18–20.
Simons, E. L. (1987). "New fossil apes from Egypt and the initial differences of Hominoidea." *Primate Evolution and Human Origins*. R. a. J. G. F. Ciochon. New York, Aldine De Gruyter: 145–150.
Smith, J. M. (1996). *Did Darwin get it right? But is it Science?: the Philosophical Question in the Creation/Evolution Controversy*. M. Ruse. New York, Prometheus Books: 195–201.
Stein, P. L. a. B. M. R. (1998). *Physical Anthropology: The Core*. Boston, WCB McGraw-Hill.
Stephan, H., G. Buron, and H. Frahm. (1988). "Comparative size of brains and brain components." *Comparative Primate Biology Vol. 4 Neuroscience*. H. Steklis, and J. Erwin. New York, Alan R. Liss: 1–38.
Strickland, G. G. (1979). *Genesis Revisited: a Revolutionary New Solution to the Mystery of Man's Origins*. New York, Dial Press.
Svitil, K. A. (2002). "Did Viruses Make Us Human?" *Discover* 23(11): 10.
Tattersall, I., E. Delson, and J.A. Van Couvering. (1988). *Encyclopedia of Human Evolution and Prehistory*. New York, Garland.
Tattersall, I. (1995). *The Fossil Trail: How We Know What We Think We Know About Human Evolution*. New York, Oxford University Press.
Teilhard de Chardin, P. (1965). *The Appearance of Man*. New York, Harper & Row Publishers.

Thomas and R. J. Blackwell (1963). *Commentary on Aristotle's Physics*. New Haven, Yale University Press.

Turnbaugh, W. A., R.Jurmain, H Nelson, and L. Kilgore. (1996). *Understanding Physical Anthropology and Archaeology*. Minnesota, West Publishing Company.

Wade, N. (2002). "In DNA, New Clues to Jewish Roots." *The New York Times*. New York: F1 and F7.

Wade, N. (2002). "Insight into Human-Chimp Differences." *The New York Times*. New York: A18.

Walsh, J. L. (1996). *Unraveling Piltdown: The Science Fraud of the Century and its Solution.* New York, Random House.

Wenke, R. J. (1990). *Patterns in Prehistory: Humankind's First Three Million Years*. New York, Oxford University Press.

White, T., Gen Suwa and Berhane Asfaw (1994). "Australopithecus Ramidus, a New Species of Early Hominid from Aramis, Ethiopia." *Nature* 371: 306–312.

Whitehead, T. L. (1980). "Identity, Subjectivity and Cultural Bias in Fieldwork." *The Black Scholar: Journal of Black Studies and Research* 11(7): 40–44, 83–87.

Whittaker, J. C. (1997*). Flintknapping: Making and Understanding Stone Tools*. Austin, University of Texas Press.

Williams, H. S. (1931). *The Biography of Mother Earth.* New York, R. M. McBride & Company.

Williams, B. A. a. R. F. K. (1994/95). "The Taxon Anthropoidea and the Crown Clade Concept." *Evolutionary Anthropology* 3(6): 188–190.

Wiredu, K. (1996). *Cultural Universals and Particulars: an African Perspective*. Bloomington, Indiana University Press.

Wireless, C. (1929). "Skeleton Called that of Earliest Modern Man is Dug Up in Kenya and Removed Intact." *The New York Times*: 9:2.

Wolpoff, M. a. R. C. (1997). *Race and Human Evolution: A Fatal Attraction*. New York, Simon and Schuster.

Wyss, A. R. a. J. J. F. (1994/95). "'Anthropoidea': A Name, Not an Entity." *Evolutionary Anthropology* 3(6): 187–188.

Zahn, T. (2001). *Angelmass*. New York, Tor.

Zanelli, J. and C. Teitelboim (1998). *The Black Hole: 25 Years After*. Singapore; River Edge, N.J., World Scientific.

Zapfe, H. (1960). "A New Fossil Anthropoid from the Miocene of Austria." *Current Anthropology* 1(5/6): 428–429.

Index

www.ingramcontent.com/pod-product-compliance
Lightning Source LLC
Chambersburg PA
CBHW020238290326
41929CB00044B/328

* 9 7 8 0 7 6 1 8 6 3 5 7 1 *